P9-DIB-626

RETURN TO THE GARDEN

RETURN TO THE GARDEN

A Journey of Discovery

BY
SHAKTI GAWAIN

NEW WORLD LIBRARY
SAN RAFAEL, CALIFORNIA

© 1989 Shakti Gawain
Published by New World Library
58 Paul Drive, San Rafael,
California 94903

Cover art by Mark Reynolds
Cover design by Kathleen Vande Kieft
Text design by Nancy Benedict
Illustrations by Michael Stillwater
Back cover photo by Elizabeth Gawain
Typography by Walker Graphics/Techtron

All rights reserved. This book may not be re-produced in whole or in part, without written permission from the publisher, except by a reviewer who may quote brief passages in a review; nor may any part of this book be reproduced, stored in a retrieval system, or transmitted in any form or by any means electronic, mechanical, photocopying, recording, or other, without written permission from the publisher.

First hardcover printing, September, 1989

ISBN 0-931432-88-X

This book is dedicated to our mother,
the Earth.

CONTENTS

THREE

FOUR

ACKNOWLEDGMENTS

I would like to thank the following people for their help in creating and preparing this book: Kathryn Altman, Marc Allen, Carol LaRusso, Katherine Dieter, Cheryl White, and Deborah Eaglebarger. Special thanks goes to my friend Manuela for her constant support and assistance on every level.

I appreciate the suggestions and feedback given by Leslie Ayvazian, Jonathan Merritt, Tanha, Kathleen Holland, Hal Stone and Sidra Winkelman, Beth Gawain, Thomas Weinberg, Joanna Karp, and other good friends.

I want to acknowledge my family, friends, lovers, staff, students, clients, and readers—all of you who have contributed so much to my life and therefore to this book. Some of you are mentioned by name in the book, others are not. My desire was to include and acknowledge every person whom I have ever known and cared for. However, that was simply not practical; the book would have been at least a thousand pages long! For simplicity and clarity, I have had to focus on certain themes, incidents, and people. Some of you may feel left out, whereas others of you may *wish* you had been left out! Whether or not you are specifically mentioned you know who you are, and I hope you know what you have given to me. I thank you and I love you.

DEAR READERS

I'm sitting in a comfortable, naturally hollowed-out throne on a large black lava rock formation projecting out into the blue ocean from a beautiful white sand beach. This is my power spot, the place in the whole world where I feel most connected with my soul. In front of me, waves roll in from the open sea, carrying vast oceans of intense energy. They break right in front of me, showering me with their life force. Underneath me the rock is warm and smooth and as powerful in its solidity as the ocean is in its movement. The combination of still rock and moving water brings me into absolute balance and wholeness. I live near here now, so I can come here often. When I'm here, I often feel that my soul is talking to me, telling me things I need to remember. And sometimes I feel the earth is talking to me, too.

How did I come to this beautiful place? That, among other things, is what this book is about.

I needed to write this book for two reasons. First, I wanted to talk about my feelings about the earth. This is a very important time in our planet's history. We are beginning to wake up and become aware of our relationship to the earth and to all of earth's creatures. It is time for us to learn to live naturally and harmoniously as conscious beings on the earth, integrating our spiritual beings with our physical selves. This book is my offering toward that quest.

The second reason for writing this book is to tell you my personal story. My previous books (and parts of this one) are channeled from my highest creative source and are primarily focused on explaining how we can live in accordance with simple universal principles.

Often when people who have read my books meet me, I find they have put me on a pedestal and expect me to be radiant and perfect. They are quite shocked to find that I am a human being more or less like everyone else, struggling to integrate my spiritual wisdom with my very human personality. At moments I am quite clear and radiant, at other moments I am an emotional basket case, and most of the time I am somewhere in between. It's lonely on a pedestal. I'm sharing my story with you because I want to be known as a person. It makes me feel vulnerable to tell you about my life because I'm opening myself to the possibility of being judged and/or misunderstood. Yet I know that many of you will appreciate and relate to what I am sharing. And I need to tell my story, so here it is.

This book is about my personal journey of discovery and my return to the garden of my own soul and my connection to the earth. And it is also about the possibility of humanity returning to the garden, living life on earth in a natural and balanced way.

My wish is that in sharing my adventures, my struggles, my frustrations and victories, my pain and my joy, you will find much that will comfort and inspire you on your own journey.

With love,

Shakti

ONE

EARTH'S JOURNEY

THE GARDEN
(A Short History of the World)

Once, in a place beyond time and space, a consciousness existed in a state of oneness and bliss. This consciousness came to realize it also wanted to experience twoness, or duality. In this way it could experience the excitement of splitting into opposite polarities, and the ecstasy of merging back into one.

So original consciousness (which we can call Spirit, or God, or Source), while still remaining one, also created itself into two opposite energies which we can call yin and yang, or female and male, or dark and light, or spirit and form. The yang, or masculine force, would always pull toward action, individuation, separation, difference. The yin, or feminine force, would always pull toward being, merging, union, oneness. Life became the dance of the continuous pulsation between these energies. Each time the male and female energies met, a new creation was born.

From this dance physical form was created. The pull of the masculine force toward individuation created a dense physical world in which each form was separate and distinct from every other form. Of course, all the forms were created out of the same original energy, so the feminine force constantly pulled them back toward experiencing the energetic vibration of their oneness. The yang pushed toward constant birth of new forms, the yin moved toward death of form and surrender back into the whole.

The physical world that was created from this dance of energies was astounding. There was a vast cosmos filled with blazing suns and countless planets. One small planet, which would become known as Earth, was unbelievably rich and beautiful. She was a lush, magical garden with vast, deep oceans, dense jungles, green forests, and white deserts. Spirit had created itself into many wondrous forms of plants and other living creatures on Earth.

The yin and yang energies began to create two separate kinds of forms—male and female. Each form contained both energies, but outwardly manifested more of the qualities of one than the other. The male forms expressed more aggressive, outward-moving energies. The female forms expressed more receptive, inward-moving energies. When the two united, a new being was created.

All kinds of new and interesting creatures developed. Some of the older forms remained undifferentiated male and female all in one, but many of the newer types were divided into males and females. The garden flourished and was abundant with millions of species of plants, insects, fish, and animals, all living in balance and harmony in an explosion of creativity.

Then a new kind of creature developed, known as a human being. The one who represented the male polarity was called Man; the one who represented the female polarity was called Woman. As a whole, their species had a stronger male energy than any previous creature, and because of this they had a new feature—a rational mind that could make all kinds of distinctions and separations.

For a while, Man and Woman dwelt happily in the garden in a childlike state of innocence and wonder. They lived spontaneously in each moment, experiencing life deeply and fully and with great feeling. They loved each other passionately, for each recognized in the other a mirror of the opposite polarity they carried within themselves. Man knew he contained a female aspect within him and Woman was aware of the male aspect of herself. They realized they were expressions of the two aspects of God, and they delighted in their own beauty and power. They spent their days frolicking with the other creatures in the garden, loving each other, and learning about existence. But a strange fate awaited them.

One day a beautiful and wise creature known as Snake came to Woman. He told her that humankind had a powerful and unique destiny. Through them, the Universal Source would explore the farthest limits of the masculine polarity—the principle of individuation and separation. Snake said that Spirit needed to develop its masculine principle of action and individuality as strongly as it had already developed its feminine principle of being and oneness. Only with an equally strong male and female could the universe eventually make love to itself in endless ecstatic union.

Snake said that Man and Woman would have to leave their innocent, delightful life in the garden, and venture deeper into the physical world. They needed to explore physical existence to the fullest. In order to do so they would have to temporarily forget their spiritual selves and become almost totally lost in and preoccupied with the material world. He told her that the physical plane would come to feel much more real than the spiritual. Man and Woman and their descendants would become the masters of the material world. The knowledge and power they would gain from their experiences would be incredible. The danger was that they would eventually have the power of destruction to match the power of creation they already had, gaining the ability to destroy themselves and the entire physical world.

If they were able to meet their challenges successfully, the wisdom and maturity they would gain would be invaluable. They would become fully integrated, balanced spiritual/physical beings, channeling the full creative power of the universe into the physical world. They would re-create life in the garden on Earth, more beautiful than ever. They would return to the garden of innocence, love, and wonder, but this time with the wisdom of experience and the power to protect it and take care of it forever.

Snake told Woman that the journey would be hard and long and a great challenge, but the rewards could be equally great. They would have to leave the garden and find their own way. He said all the other creatures on Earth would be helping them, although Man and Woman would not remember that. Then he pointed to a certain tree known as the Tree of Knowledge. It had beautiful juicy-looking fruit, but for some reason no one had ever eaten any of it. Snake told Woman she must convince Man to eat some. Then he disappeared.

Woman was heavy-hearted, intuitively sensing what lay before her. But she knew she must do as advised. She had no trouble convincing Man to eat the fruit. He loved and trusted her completely, knowing her to truly be the reflection of the female energy within himself, so he ate the delicious fruit as she suggested.

Immediately, everything shifted.

Man and Woman no longer felt the bliss and safety of the magical garden. Suddenly their minds felt very sharp, and they began to question everything. "Where am I? Why am I here?" Rather than living in just the present moment, they became vividly aware of the past and the future. "Where have I been? What should I do next?" They began to question and analyze everything and to notice all kinds of distinctions and differences.

Although their surroundings remained the same, they saw and felt everything differently. Their world seemed duller, as if their senses were perceiving less vividly. Nothing looked quite perfect anymore. They felt frightened and alone.

Worst of all they felt differently about themselves and each other. They became very self-conscious. Instead of feeling like natural god-like beings, they now felt inadequate and foolish. Instead of loving and trusting each other as aspects of themselves, they noticed how different they were and felt suspicious of one another. Once they realized they were physically different, they felt embarrassed about being naked, and made clothes out of leaves and put them on.

They felt hungry and worried about how they were going to survive, so they set out to find food and shelter. Although they vaguely remembered life in the Garden, the memory gradually faded as they became preoccupied with learning about survival in this new reality. They forgot that they were God's spirit in physical form, and began to think of God as someone very far away who might or might not help them in their struggles. They created some rituals which momentarily brought back the blissful feeling of being one with God, but most of the time they felt separate and alone.

Still, they became fascinated with the task of learning to live in the physical world. They learned how to gather fruits and nuts and hunt animals for food. The climate had changed when they left the Garden, and because it was often very cold, they discovered how to use animal skins for clothing, and caves for shelter.

Man and Woman began to divide their tasks. Since Man was physically stronger he went out to hunt, while Woman gathered and prepared food and maintained their shelter.

While being conscious of their differences made them feel uncomfortable with each other, at the same time their polarization made them very attracted to each other. They had forgotten that they were each whole within themselves. Each felt the other had something he or she lacked, and needed desperately. Their need for one another frightened them. They didn't like the feeling that each one had so much power over the other, so they tried to hide their feelings. They became distrustful of each other, yet they couldn't help longing to be close.

The only way they knew how to express this yearning toward one another was through sexual union. When they had sex, they felt that old familiar ecstatic feeling they used to experience continuously when they lived in the Garden. The feeling passed quickly, however, and their attention turned once again to important matters of survival.

One fascinating result of their sexual experiences was that they began to have children! It was amazing and exciting to discover that they had the power together to create new human beings similar to themselves. Yet it was worrisome, too, because it meant more mouths to feed and more responsibilities.

Their children grew up and had children. Man and Woman discovered that their physical bodies were changing—they were slowly wearing out! As their bodies grew slower and more tired, and their grown children took over most of the work, they found more leisure time. They took walks in the forest, and sat together and watched the sunset. It stirred ancient memories of their joyous time together in the Garden. The everyday concerns of the world no longer seemed so important. In fact, they began to forget a lot of irrelevant details, like the names of all their children, or what year it was. They loved being with their little grandchildren, though. In their innocent young faces, so filled with spontaneous feeling in each moment, Man and Woman saw the mirror of their own souls, which they had long forgotten. Through the beauty of nature and the reflection from their children's children, they found and reunited with the pure essence of their beings. Soon, their souls passed from their physical forms and moved to another level of reality.

The grandchildren of Man and Woman grew up and lost their innocence, as they, too, faced the cares and challenges of the world. With each succeeding generation it was the same. For a brief time in infancy, it was as if each being dwelt momentarily in the Garden, and perceived the world with fresh new eyes of love and wonder and oneness with all life. And then each person set about to define him- or herself as a separate and unique human being, and to discover how to survive and grow in what often came to seem like an unfriendly and difficult world.

Many hundreds and thousands of generations passed, and despite countless difficulties and disasters, humankind as a whole developed and prospered and spread all over Earth. They learned to grow food and developed more and more efficient ways to farm. They discovered better and better ways to make tools and weapons so that they could defend their territory or take over someone else's. They built bigger and fancier shelters; eventually some were so huge that they were taller than any tree and could hold hundreds of people!

True to Snake's prediction, after many, many centuries, human beings had become masters of the physical world. They had created a sophisticated technology that could accomplish all kinds of amazing and seemingly magical feats. They could propel human beings from Earth into space and return them safely (most of the time). They had ships that could dive into the depths of the ocean and return safely to the surface (most of the time). A human being on one side of Earth could speak to a human being on the other side of Earth just by talking into a little gadget called a telephone (unless they got "a bad connection").

People could talk or play music and millions of others all over the world could see and hear them on a box called a television. And people could travel hundreds or thousands of miles in a few minutes or hours in strange creatures called automobiles and airplanes, which gulped strong-smelling liquids and then bellowed out fumes.

As Snake had promised Woman, the plants, animals, and other creatures on Earth helped humanity in its endeavors. Certain species of plants and animals had even sacrificed themselves to become food, companions, and workers for the human race. Unfortunately, most human beings did not recognize or appreciate this. They had become extremely arrogant, almost blind in their relationship to Earth and her other creatures, and they saw themselves as superior to everyone and everything else on Earth. They felt it their duty and their right to conquer and control everything around them. In their quest for mastery of the physical universe, they had completely lost touch with many of the simple, natural laws of Earth that had kept everything functioning harmoniously.

As a result, Earth's systems became severely out of balance and life on earth for human beings and all other creatures deteriorated rapidly. Humans had proliferated so greatly that there were just too many of them to live comfortably on the planet. A great number of humans lived in crowded concrete jungles of buildings, called cities, where there was little contact with the nurturing, comforting elements of nature. Life was dreary and often dangerous and violent in these jungles. The air and the food were filled with poisons, so people were actually destroying themselves as they breathed and ate!

Vast amounts of Earth's resources—land and water all over the world—were used to grow feed for animals who were then slaughtered to feed the wealthiest people in small areas of the world. These people sometimes destroyed large amounts of food to keep things in what they called "economic balance." Meanwhile, increasing numbers of poor people in these same areas, and even more all over the world, were actually starving to death!

Ultimately, large areas of Earth became polluted. Many rivers and lakes and even the vast oceans were being destroyed by chemicals used routinely by humans in their farming and manufacturing endeavors.

Many species of plants and animals were destroyed by man's activities. Many other magnificent creatures grew close to extinction as human civilization expanded heedlessly into previously pristine areas.

Even the weather on Earth began to change dramatically, altered by human beings' experiments on earth and in space, and by the destruction of the tropical rain forests.

As Snake had warned, the human species had indeed developed the power of destruction. Not only were they destroying Earth through their careless lack of attunement to one another and to Earth as a whole, they actually set about to create the most violent, destructive weapons they could, and succeeded extremely well at the task. They had systems in which a few people could push buttons that would instantly unleash enough power to destroy the entire Earth and all her living creatures!

Like small boys playing with their Christmas toys, the humans experimented with the first versions of these powerful weapons, and they destroyed many other people and scared themselves quite a bit in the process. So they put the weapons on the shelf, but kept building bigger and stronger ones and putting those on the shelf as well. They loved to threaten each other with them, and were always trying to figure out who had the most potential destructive power.

The human beings were in a sad state spiritually and emotionally. As Snake had predicted, humans had gone so deeply into the consciousness of the physical plane that they had become lost in that reality. They had forgotten their origin as divine, loving, powerful spiritual beings.

Because they had disconnected themselves from the power of Spirit, at their emotional core they felt helpless, frightened, and alone. They became preoccupied with trying to gain material power in the world, thinking this would make them feel safe and secure. Many of them became obsessed with money, success, status, and political influence.

Because human beings were disconnected from the fullness of Spirit, feeling empty and dissatisfied, they became engrossed in trying to find some kind of fulfillment in external things. They became addicted to food, alcohol and other drugs, sex, or other pursuits that could give them a temporary feeling of pleasure or satisfaction.

Because they had lost touch with their own inner nature, and with the natural world around them, they lost much of their intuitive understanding about relating to one another. And since many humans were so emotionally deprived and out of balance, they had great difficulty raising their children in a healthy way. The environments they had created were not very conducive to the nurturing of children, either.

Many young humans were not getting their emotional needs met, and were growing up frightened, sad, angry, frustrated, or emotionally numb. They, in turn, passed these qualities on to their children.

Throughout the ages there had always been a few human beings who retained their connection to Spirit, and who recognized the imbalances in the world. Some of them had tried to bring awareness to others, in various ways and with varying degrees of success. Now, because of the increasing severity of the situation, more people were becoming aware of the problems and were searching for solutions. Many were seeking truth through exploring the creative arts. Some explored human psychology in order to heal themselves and each other emotionally. Others worked on political and environmental issues. And some, in search of spiritual answers, turned toward ancient teachings, reinterpreted them for modern times, and shared them with others.

Many of these truthseekers found that their lives were improving. Their spiritual practices helped them feel more and more connected with their Source and they began to feel the power of God moving through them to heal some of the problems in their lives and in the world. Sometimes they observed miraculous things happening through this creative power they channeled.

The psychological work they did helped them clear away a lot of the old misconceptions and emotional patterns that had been handed down through generations. Those who had the courage to face their greatest fear and pain moved through their deepest darkness and found the light.

They began to love and accept themselves and each other again. They learned to accept and enjoy their human feelings and emotions, and to communicate with each other more honestly. This helped them find more of the closeness and intimacy they needed in their relationships with each other. Some men started to realize that the women in their lives mirrored the female energy within themselves, while some women began to recognize the men in their lives as the reflection of their own inner male energies.

All of this helped them to appreciate each other more. As they gained more confidence in the wholeness within themselves, they felt less powerless and less frightened of each other. They became more comfortable with the tremendous attraction they felt between them, recognizing it as the natural dance between the female and male polarities of the universe. Once they felt better about themselves and each other, they were more able to love and nurture the children they gave birth to. They began to recognize in their children the innocent, spontaneous essence they had lost touch with in themselves, and they allowed their children to teach them about reuniting with their own inner selves.

In turn, they were finally able to model for their children how to live effectively and happily in the physical world. The new beings being born into bodies no longer had to go through the pain of forgetting who they were and feeling lost, but were recognized from conception and birth as spiritual beings, and encouraged to live and express their truth. Open and clear, channeling a great deal of creative power, many of them seemed to know their life purpose and began to move toward it at a young age.

The truthseekers tried to solve some of the political, social, and environmental problems around them. A few of them were even elected or appointed to political office. Others wrote books and articles or created movies or television programs to try to wake people up. Many simply worked hard to deal with individual problems in their communities. In some cases, wonderful progress was made; other times it was discouraging.

The number of truthseekers was small though steadily growing, but overall conditions on Earth were becoming worse for most people. There was increasing violence and insanity among humans. Most of the political leaders, reflecting the masses, were still trying to do things in the same old way. Pollution and ecological destruction were rampant. The Earth herself was angry and upset, and demonstrated her desire for respect through earthquakes, volcanoes, floods, climactic change, and other means at her disposal.

The souls of many humans and other creatures, recognizing the degree of transformation that was called for and not desiring to go through all the effort, chose to go through the transition called "death," and departed from their physical bodies. They went on to experience another level of existence for a while, some of them feeling that perhaps they would come back to this physical reality again later on when it got a little easier or more pleasurable.

Those who remained, whether or not they were consciously aware of it, were determinedly adventurous types who wanted to be part of the dramatic change that was taking place.

As outward conditions continued to grow darker, increasing numbers of humans were driven inward, looking for some light. They were forced out of their numb state of denial, and began facing their fear and pain. More and more of them became truthseekers.

The new teachings spread, through speakers, books, movies, and even television (the bastion of the old reality). People began to gather into small groups everywhere on Earth, sharing their fears and problems and giving each other support and inspiration. They realized that none of them could solve their difficulties alone—they needed each other's assistance and love. From these gatherings new tribes gradually formed, made up of people who realized their spiritual connection to one another and their mission together. Different tribes worked in different ways but they shared a similar purpose—to serve God by saving themselves and the planet.

Some of these tribes of truthseekers found themselves drawn to certain powerful places on the earth. They migrated and settled in these special power spots. Here they recognized Earth herself as their mother and their greatest teacher. They surrendered their lives to her, and asked her to guide them in learning to live naturally, in truth and harmony.

Thus humankind, which had fulfilled its destiny to carry the polarity of male energy to its extreme of individuation and separation, was coming full circle. Once again humans were returning to the power of the feminine principle and embracing her.

Earth responded like any loving mother to her children, embracing the humans with an abundance of nurturing, love, and wisdom. She began to talk to them in many ways and teach them everything they needed to know. They began to practice rituals of meditation, singing, and dancing to attune themselves to Earth. With her support they reconnected with the ancient wisdom they carried in their souls. Step by step, Earth taught them how to live naturally and in a balanced way. They found healing for their bodies, emotions, minds, and spirits. They lived in increasing honesty and acceptance with themselves and one another. They grew and ate food that was natural and nourishing to them in ways that followed Earth's natural laws. They built shelters that were comfortable, beautiful, and that blended with the surrounding environment. They created schools that were fun and exciting for their children and taught them all the things they needed to know about living. They reformed local political systems and elected leaders who upheld their values. They committed themselves to solving local ecological and environmental problems, while also working to influence larger world issues.

They also created healing and teaching centers. Many people came from all over the world to receive personal healing on all levels and to learn all aspects of this new way of life. They would stay for a certain period of time, undergo great personal transformation, and then return to their homes to teach and heal others. In this way, the new way was carried from the power spots to many places on Earth.

Certain people who came for healing were very powerful in the old world. Some of them were influential in the media, and once they realized the transformation that was possible, they began to send the message out to the world. They created some popular television programs that carried the message in an interesting and entertaining way, and since millions of people were plugged into the global network of television, the vision of a new way of life was effectively spread everywhere. New leaders were elected who were committed to their own personal transformation and to the creation of a new world. With guidance from the Higher Power and support from the people and all the creatures of Earth, they dissolved or changed the old institutions that were no longer working and created new ones that worked effectively for the highest good of all.

The human species stopped polluting and destroying the earth. They learned to live on her in balance and love. Gradually, Earth began flourishing again and grew more beautiful than ever before.

Human beings lived spontaneously, finding in each moment the pleasure and fulfillment of growth, change, and aliveness. They felt a part of the Great Spirit that unified all life and all existence. At the same time they appreciated their individual differences and loved themselves, including their human limitations. They looked at the world with innocent freshness in each moment, yet remembered their past pain. Their experience brought them the wisdom and strength to protect and care for themselves and for the Earth.

Men and women loved each other passionately and were not afraid to feel the intensity of their love. They saw the beauty and power of the entire universe reflected in one another, and in their children. They lived in harmony with the Earth, with all the Earth's creatures and with all the rhythms of nature.

Humankind had returned to the Garden.

LEARNING FROM THE EARTH

The Earth is our mother. She has been the nurturing mother who cares for her infants and provides them with everything they need. As her babies grew into young children, she sat back patiently and allowed us to explore and learn to do things for ourselves. She allowed us to make our mistakes, even when they were hurtful to her, knowing that was the only way we could learn and develop. And she was always there when we needed her, like a mother whose child toddles away from her to explore the world, then comes running back to her lap when it needs comfort and reassurance.

Now we are growing up. It is time for us to take responsibility for our own behavior. Earth, loving us as much as ever, is now taking a more stern tone, knowing this is for our good as well as her own. She cannot allow us to continue carelessly making messes and not bothering to clean them up. We can no longer live in childish egocentricity, without regard for the other beings around us. Earth is becoming a stricter mother. Just as every child needs to have some limits set in order to learn how to live in the world with respect for others, Earth is now making clear to us what her personal boundaries are, and she is insisting that we respect them.

As our mother, Earth is also our best teacher. If we pay attention, we can learn from her everything we need to know about how to live on the physical plane. Every day, in every way, she demonstrates to us her natural rhythms and cycles, all the natural laws of life.

Her other children, our older brothers and sisters—the plants and animals—are important teachers as well. They already live in attunement with Mother Earth. By following their example we can learn many things about ourselves.

Some of our other older siblings, many of the ancient peoples, also understood their place as part of the great family of Earth. We can learn much by studying their ways and bringing forward those ideas and practices which can help us. Not that we need to, or can, return to the past, but within their way of life was and still is great wisdom, which we with our vast sophisticated knowledge have lost. We must find that innate wisdom again, and use our technical knowledge not to destroy but to enhance and protect the Earth.

Here is a beautiful example of the great wisdom of the past. It is a letter written in the early 1850's by Chief Seattle of the Suwamish tribe, in what is now the state of Washington, to President Franklin Pierce of the United States in response to an offer made for a large area of Native American land, and a promise to provide them with a reservation.

How can you buy or sell the sky, the warmth of the land? The idea is strange to us. If we do not own the freshness of the air and the sparkle of the water, how can you buy them?

Every part of the earth is sacred to my people.

Every shining pine needle, every sandy shore, every mist in the dark woods, every clearing and humming insect is holy in the memory and experience of my people. The sap which courses through the trees carries the memories of the red man.

The white man's dead forget the country of their birth when they go to walk among the stars. Our dead never forget this beautiful earth for it is the mother of the red man.

We are part of the earth and it is part of us.

The perfumed flowers are our sisters; the deer, the horse, the great eagle, these are our brothers.

The rocky crests, the juices in the meadows, the body heat of the pony, the man—all belong to the same family.

So, when the Great Chief in Washington sends word that he wishes to buy our land, he asks much of us. The Great Chief sends word he will reserve us a place so that we can live comfortably to ourselves.

He will be our father and we will be his children. So we will consider your offer to buy our land.

But it will not be easy. For this land is sacred to us.

The shining water that moves in the streams and rivers is not just water but the blood of our ancestors.

If we sell our land, you must remember that it is sacred, and you must teach your children that it is sacred and that each ghostly reflection in the clear water of the lakes tells of events and memories in the life of my people. The water's murmur is the voice of my father's father.

The rivers are our brothers, they quench our thirst. The rivers carry our canoes, and feed our children. If we sell our land, you must remember, and teach your children, that the rivers are our brothers, and yours, and you must henceforth give the rivers the kindness you would give any brother.

We know that the white man does not understand our ways. One portion of the land is the same to him as the next, for he is a stranger who comes in the night and takes from the land whatever he needs.

The earth is not his brother, but his enemy, and when he has conquered it, he moves on.

He leaves his father's grave behind, and he does not care. He kidnaps the earth from his children, and he doesn't care.

His father's grave and his childrens' birthrights are forgotten. He treats his mother the earth and his brother the sky as things to be bought, plundered, sold like sheep or bright beads.

I do not know. Our ways are different from your ways. The sight of your cities pains the eyes of the red man. But perhaps it is because the red man is a savage and does not understand.

There is no quiet place in the white man's cities. No

place to hear the unfurling of leaves in the spring, or the rustle of an insect's wings.

But perhaps it is because I'm a savage and do not understand.

The clatter only seems to insult the ears. And what is there to life if a man cannot hear the lonely cry of the whippoorwill or the arguments of the frogs around the pond at night? I am a red man and do not understand.

The indian prefers the soft sound of the wind darting over the face of a pond, and the smell of the wind itself, cleaned by a midday rain, or scented with the pinon pine.

The air is precious to the red man, for all things share the same breath—the beast, the tree, the man, they all share the same breath.

The white man does not seem to notice the air he breathes. Like a man dying for many days, he is numb to the stench.

But if we sell our land, you must remember that the air is precious to us, that the air shares its spirit with all the life it supports. The wind that gave our grandfather his first breath also receives his last sigh.

And if we sell our land, you must keep it apart and sacred, as a place where even the white man can go to taste the wind that is sweetened by the meadow's flowers.

So we will consider your offer to buy our land. If we decide to accept, I will make one condition: the white man must treat the beasts of this land as his brothers.

I'm a savage and I do not understand any other way. What is man without the beasts? If all the beasts were gone, man would die from a great loneliness of spirit.

For whatever happens to the beasts soon happens to man. All things are connected.

You must teach your children that the ground beneath their feet is the ashes of your grandfathers. So that they will respect the land, tell your children that the earth is rich with the lives of our kin.

Teach your children what we have taught our children, that the earth is our mother.

Whatsoever befalls the earth befalls the sons of the earth. If men spit upon the ground, they spit upon themselves.

I have seen a thousand buffalo rotting on the prairie, left by the white man who shot them from a passing train.

I am a savage and I do not understand how the smoking iron horse can be more important than the buffalo that we kill only to stay alive.

This we know: the earth does not belong to man; man belongs to the earth. This we know.

All things are connected like the blood which unites one family. All things are connected.

Whatever befalls the earth befalls the sons of the earth. Man did not weave the web of life; he is merely a strand in it. Whatever he does to the web he does to himself.

Even the white man, whose God walks and talks with him as friend to friend, cannot be exempt from the common destiny.

We may be brothers after all. We shall see.

One thing we know, which the white man may one day discover—our God is the same God.

You may think now that you own Him as you wish to own our land; but you cannot. He is the God of man, and His compassion is equal for the red man and the white.

The earth is precious to Him, and to harm the earth is to heap contempt on its Creator.

The whites too shall pass; perhaps sooner than all other tribes. Contaminate your bed, and you will one night suffocate in your own waste.

But in your perishing you will shine brightly, fired by the strength of the God who brought you to this land and for some special purpose gave you domination over this land and over the red man.

That destiny is a mystery to us, for we do not understand what will happen when the buffalo are all slaughtered and the horses are all tamed, when the secret corners of the forest are heavy with the scent of many men, and the view of ripe hills is blotted by talking wires.

Where is the thicket? Gone.

Where is the eagle? Gone.

The ending of living and the beginning of survival.

When the last Red Man has vanished with his wilderness and his memory is only the shadow of a cloud moving across the prairie, will these shores and forests still be here? Will there be any of the spirit of my people left?

We love this earth as a newborn loves its mother's heartbeat.

So, if we sell our land, love it as we have loved it. Care for it as we have cared for it. Hold in your mind the memory of the land as it is when you receive it. Preserve the land for all children and love it, as God loves us all.

As we are part of the land, you too are part of the land. This earth is precious to us.

One thing we know: there is only one God. No man, be he Red Man or White Man, can be apart.

We *are* brothers after all.

A TURNING POINT

We have reached a crucial time in the history of the world. We human beings have a natural propensity toward exploration and adventure, a tendency to move constantly outward into the farthest reaches of the unknown. I see this as an expression of the male principle in the universe—an aggressive movement from the known center outward to discover and conquer new territory, both physically and mentally.

This drive to explore and create has served us well. Through it, we have discovered whole new worlds. We have created a technology so miraculous that it puts us in the realm of the gods. We have developed and unleashed extraordinary power.

All of this was necessary and important. I believe our mission was to develop the male principle of action and individuation to its greatest extent, to fully empower it so that it could match and balance the powerful female principle of being and merging. In order to do so, we had to experience the polarity that is completely opposite from our sense of oneness. We had to feel separate and alone, we had to find our own way in order to develop our own sense of power. We had to take it to the extreme, go way out of balance.

In moving so far away from our center, we almost completely lost touch with that center, with our spiritual origin and source. Engrossed in our masculine task, we lost contact with the power of the feminine principle. Our world was focused on the goals and priorities of our male energies, without the equal balance of our feminine priorities.

I don't believe this is a bad thing, or a giant mistake, but instead a necessary step in our evolution. From a metaphysical perspective, it had to happen this way.

Now, however, we have reached a turning point. If we continue to progress in the same direction we will go too far out of balance. The universal system will need to right itself, and it will do so naturally through our own self-destruction and possibly the destruction of our entire planet.

In my view, the pendulum has begun to swing back in the other direction. The power of the female principle embodied in Earth herself is once again on the rise. The goddess is and will be demanding our respect and support. This does not mean we need to honor the feminine energies and values above the masculine. It is time for them to come into *equality* and *balance* in the physical world. We each need to honor the power of the female and male aspects within ourselves and in the world around us.

We can do this by learning to feel and trust the intuitive feminine power within each of us and supporting it with our masculine power of action in the physical world. As we practice listening to our intuition and acting on it, moment by moment in every aspect of our daily lives, we bring the female and male sides of our nature into integration and alignment. As more and more individuals live this way, we bring the world into balance.

More people are beginning to turn inward to search for that which has been lost in our focus on external progress. Some are studying ancient teachings and practices to rediscover the spiritual tools we need now. Others are delving into the modern science of psychology to learn how to live in a healthy and natural way. Many are awakening to the extremely serious problems we have created in our world environment, and are dedicating themselves to finding practical solutions.

Yet the mass consciousness is still moving with great momentum in the old direction. Each one of us is a part of that mass consciousness. It's time for every one of us who is awake and aware at this time to make a firm commitment to our own physical, emotional, mental, and spiritual healing, and to the healing of our planet.

FACING OUR SHADOW

One of the most important aspects of healing ourselves and the earth is the willingness to face our "shadow"—the feelings and parts of ourselves that we have rejected, repressed, or disowned. Our society has tremendous prohibitions against feeling too much. We are afraid to feel too much fear, hurt, sadness, or anger, and oftentimes we are also afraid to feel too much love, passion, or joy! And we're definitely afraid of our natural sensuality and sexuality.

As children we learn to reject and repress these unacceptable feelings and parts of ourselves. Most of us are encouraged either to repress our vulnerable feelings and become strong and powerful, or to repress our power and aggression and be gentle and vulnerable. Or we may repress both vulnerability and power (as well as sexuality, of course) and become nice, safe, middle-of-the-roaders. In any case we lose not only major parts of our personality and being, but an enormous amount of our life force.

The feelings and parts of ourselves that we have repressed do not go away just because we don't want them. They are necessary parts of us, parts we actually need for our survival. If they are not allowed their natural expression, they go underground and fester inside of us, building up steam, needing eventual release. If we do not find ways to express them, they begin to "leak out" in distorted ways, or they begin to lead us into life situations which will give them a chance to emerge. For example, if you have repressed your power, you will have anger building up inside of you. If you don't find a way to express your anger in a direct, constructive way, it will leak out as indirect, covert hostility, or it will eventually burst forth as explosive rage or violence. It might well attract you toward angry people, with the unconscious intention of triggering your own anger.

If attempts to find expression fail or are blocked, the repressed feelings will eventually make your body sick. It is my belief that most illnesses are caused by repressed or disowned energies within us.

Personal healing on all levels—physical, emotional, mental, and spiritual—comes when we get in touch with our disowned energies. As we begin to accept them as vital part of ourselves, we begin to find safe, constructive modes of expression. Once we get to know these parts of ourselves, we find they are not as scary as we had imagined. In fact, when they are expressed and integrated, they take their place as important facets of our nature. Through integrating all aspects of ourselves, we become whole.

Everything in the universe, including every part of ourselves, wants love and acceptance. Anything in life that we don't accept will simply make trouble for us until we make peace with it. Once we do, the trouble is over.

Here is an image I have found useful to illustrate this point: Suppose you lived in a large mansion, but only occupied a few of the rooms. These rooms are bright, clean, and nicely furnished and decorated. You lead a reasonably good life in them. However, you never enter any of the other rooms in the mansion because you have been told there may be frightening things in them. You keep all the doors in the unoccupied part of the house locked and spend a lot of time worrying about what might escape from the dark part of the house into your safe area. At night you imagine all kinds of noises. A great deal of your life energy is taken up with worrying and defending yourself.

Finally you become tired of living this way, and decide to take control of the situation and examine some of the rooms. Perhaps you ask a trusted friend or two to come with you, so you will feel safer. You take a big, bright lantern and venture into the first unknown room. You find some unattractive, old-fashioned furniture, cobwebs, and a few beautiful antiques. Once you clean up the room, give away the things you don't need, and decorate it to enhance the treasures you've found, you have another unique and beautiful room in your home. When you are ready, you can proceed to the next room. Eventually, you will find yourself living in a large, beautiful, well-lighted mansion. Since you no longer have to spend your time defending yourself against the unknown darkness, you can turn your energy to more creative things.

In order to become "enlightened," we must shine the light of consciousness into any dark places that we have not yet explored. This is true on a planetary level as well as a personal one. Just as we individuals have repressed aspects of ourselves, the mass consciousness has disowned much of its energy. So we have a large collective shadow to explore.

In modern society, much of what has been repressed involves the energies related to the earth—our primal selves. We have identified too frequently with the masculine rational, active, work-oriented, orderly principles and denied the more feminine emotional, intuitive, sensual aspects. I believe this is why we are having an overwhelming epidemic of drug addiction—drugs release those disowned energies. These energies have to be expressed somehow, or we would not survive. The healing for our drug problems will come as we find more natural and constructive ways for society to support all of us, and young people in particular, in expressing energies that have been restricted, such as intuition, artistic creativity, sexuality, playfulness, and just "being."

We are also having difficulty right now dealing with our natural aggressive energy. In previous times, societies channeled this energy through great numbers of men engaging in warfare. In modern times, this is increasingly dangerous and unacceptable. Aggression is frowned upon in civilized society, except in a few sanctioned ways—through sports or business. So we have our leaders toying frustratedly with their weapons systems, not daring to use them but not willing to give them up, either, and we have increasing outbreaks of violence in our cities as well. We need to find constructive ways for all of us, men *and* women, to channel our natural aggressive energy creatively.

Many people, especially those in the spiritual and new age movements, believe that we can bring peace and light to the world by focusing on the light, trying to be unconditionally loving, visualizing peace, and so forth. There is a fundamental misunderstanding here. By trying to focus only on the things we deem "positive" and ignoring or repressing the rest, we are simply perpetuating the polarization of light and dark forces. Ironically, this further distorts and empowers the very energies we are trying to avoid.

We must deeply recognize that there is no split between "spiritual" and "unspiritual," good and bad. All aspects of life are elements of the life force and facets of the divine. True healing comes from owning and accepting all of life's energies within ourselves.

Ultimately, the collective healing of our planet can only come through the personal commitment of us all as individuals, in exploring and embracing the shadow in our own lives.

TRANSFORMING THE WORLD

If each one of us who is currently aware enough to do so makes a clear commitment to our personal and planetary healing, I believe that we can transform our world into a healthy, balanced, beautiful environment. In fact, this is already happening. As more people make this commitment, we inspire others to do so as well.

Since the physical world is a creation and a reflection of our consciousness, as we change our consciousness, the physical world around us shifts to reflect that change. As our individual consciousness changes, our personal life is transformed. Since we are each a part of the mass consciousness, one change automatically shifts the mass consciousness a bit.

When one individual begins to take responsibility for his or her relationship to the earth, the mass consciousness is affected and everyone becomes a little more aware.

What is involved in making a clear commitment to ourselves and to the earth? There are six steps which I think are necessary and important. These may be done one at a time in the order given, or in any order that seems right for you. More likely, you will find that you need to work on some or all of them simultaneously. Most of you will find that you have already been doing some or all of these things. Trust yourself and follow your own sense of what is right and appropriate for you. Each person has his or her own path, different from anyone else's, and only you can find your proper path. My suggestions are given as clarification and guidelines for those who desire them.

Steps for creating transformation:

1. The first step for each of us, I feel, is to get in contact with our own inner sense of truth. We all have very reliable inner guidance which comes to us from our own higher selves. This is not as mystical as it may sound. In fact, it is very practical and reliable. It is your own deepest sense of things, your gut feeling about what's true in any given moment. Though it may take some practice to distinguish your intuition from other feelings and fears inside of you, it's something that I have found most people can learn to do fairly easily. For a specific practice, use the exercise called Connecting With Your Inner Guidance in Part Four of this book. For more information about this, I refer you to my book, *Living in the Light*, which gives clear directions for developing your ability to contact and trust your intuitive guidance.

For many people, the realization that they have a strong sense of inner truth is connected with the awareness that there is a higher power in the universe, some guiding wisdom that we are all part of and connected to. Once we begin to have an experience of that higher power (which we may call God, spirit, source, the universe, or whatever we want to call it), we can begin to call on its guidance and surrender our lives to it more and more; the more we do, the more we discover that this is simply the most effective and fulfilling way to live.

I want to stress that one does not need to believe in God or a higher power in order to begin this process. I myself did not initially. The practice of beginning to listen to and follow your own inner truth will naturally bring forth and evolve a personal belief system that works for you.

2. Begin to imagine what you really want in your life, individually and on a planetary level. Most people unconsciously spend a lot of time imagining what they are *afraid* will happen, or what they *don't* want. Visualizing and imagining what you *want* helps you get in touch with what you truly desire in life. It

frees the creative energy within you and directs it where you really want it to go. It allows the higher universal power to support you in receiving all of life's gifts. For practice, try the exercise called Envisioning the Garden in Part Four of this book. For more specific information on this process, I refer you to my book, *Creative Visualization*.

Once you have learned to visualize what you want, practice turning it over to your higher self, or the higher power of the universe, to guide you in how to create it. Don't try to figure out intellectually how to make it happen. Continue to practice following your intuition, moment by moment, and the process will unfold in the right way.

3. A third and very important step is to make a commitment to do whatever it takes for your own personal physical, emotional, mental, and spiritual healing. Many people try to skip this step because it is by far the most difficult. Yet without it, all other effort we make in any direction is ultimately futile.

The world can only be as sane and healthy as the individuals living in it. If we want to live in a balanced environment, we must find and heal what is out of balance within ourselves.

The first step in personal healing is honest self-awareness. Notice where in your life you have stuck patterns that are not allowing your life energy to flow as freely as you'd like it to. Do you have the same painful emotional issues recurring in your relationships? Do you have food, alcohol, or drug addictions? Do you struggle with money problems? Do you have chronic physical ailments? Do you work too much and/or drive yourself too hard? Are you constantly taking care of other people's needs and ignoring your own? Do you lack self-confidence and the ability to express yourself in the world? Do you repress your "negative" feelings and focus only on the "positive"? All of these are indications of underlying emotional pain which *can* be healed.

Once you've been honest with yourself about your issues, ask yourself what kind of support you need to gain more awareness and begin to shift these patterns. In the healing process, most of us need plenty of support. Yet in our society we have been trained to believe that we should be able to do everything for ourselves, and we see it as a sign of weakness to ask for help. In reality it is the opposite—it takes great strength and courage to face yourself and be willing to receive the benefit of other people's insight and reflection.

Investigate the options that are available to you. Consider individual or group therapy and/or bodywork therapy. If you suspect that you have substance or relationship addictions (a great many people do), begin attending any of the twelve-step programs, such as Alcoholics Anonymous, Narcotics Anonymous, Overeaters Anonymous, Al-Anon, or Co-dependents Anonymous. Seek help for the specific emotional and physical problems that are troubling you. Remember that the goal of self-healing is not to change yourself into a "better" person, but to learn to love yourself and express more of who you already are.

Listen to your deepest intuitive feelings about what you need and try to act on them. Let yourself explore; if something doesn't feel quite right, try something else until you find a way that works for you. The most important thing is the authentic commitment to yourself—the willingness to do whatever it takes to become a conscious person who loves yourself, and therefore has something to share with others and the world. This type of commitment is extremely powerful, and eventually it will get you where you want to go (usually not by the route you had planned!).

Remember that deep healing does not happen overnight. It's an ongoing, unfolding process that often takes years. If it seems slow to you, remember that we are transforming not only our own personal issues, but patterns that the human race has been following for centuries! And the process of healing becomes quite fascinating and rewarding in itself.

4. The fourth step is to take a look at your daily habits of eating and living. Think about how in tune they are with your real needs and with whatever you know about the needs of the earth. Be very gentle and compassionate with yourself in this process! Most of us have lots of habits that are not particularly well-attuned to our own highest good or the good of others. There

are often deep emotional reasons for what we do, and again, we usually don't change overnight.

Many times we don't really know what is good for us. Just begin to become aware and to educate yourself. For example, if you eat a lot of canned and packaged foods and throw away the containers, you might try experimenting with eating more natural grains, fruits, and vegetables, and recycling the cans and containers you use. If there are no recycling programs in your area, see if you can help set some up.

5. Look around at your community and your environment and begin to familiarize yourself with some of the political or environmental issues in your area. Don't try to tackle everything, and don't concern yourself with trying to solve the problems of the whole world. You'll just feel overwhelmed and end up doing nothing. Find out about some of the most immediate problems in your community or area. Pick a particular issue or cause that is meaningful or interesting to you, and see if you can take a step toward making a difference. Let your friends and/or family know that you are doing this and invite them to join you if they want to, but don't push them.

If you are people-oriented, and feel so inspired, get together with groups of friends to study inspiring books, watch informative television programs or videos, and discuss issues that are of concern or importance. These meetings can be focused on personal or spiritual subjects, political or environment issues, or whatever is of greatest interest to you.

Write letters to newspapers and magazines, and to your senators and representatives, expressing your views on environmental and political issues.

6. In following any of these steps, remember not to do anything out of guilt or because you think you *should*. We all have so much dreariness in our lives already from either doing or rebelling against all the things we think we should be doing.

Instead, ask yourself what you truly *desire* to do. What turns you on? Do what feels right, and that will bring you satisfaction.

The most important point of all is to live your life with passion in a way that is meaningful and fun. How can we create a world of fulfillment and joy unless we each begin to live so in each moment?

TWO

MY JOURNEY

BIRTH

I was born in New Jersey, known as the Garden State. I was the first baby my mother's obstetrician had ever delivered by natural childbirth. In those days, educated city-dwelling American women didn't have natural childbirth—they were thoroughly anesthetized during delivery, and so the babies were born drugged as well.

My mother, being the pioneer and free-thinker that she is, decided she wanted to be awake to experience the birth of her child. She read a book called *Childbirth Without Fear*, by Grantly Dick-Read, which explained that labor could be experienced as hard work but not necessarily painful if one did not resist it.

Natural childbirth was so rare in that time and place that many of the doctors, interns, and nurses in the hospital where I was born came to witness the amazing event. So I was born to a crowd of fascinated onlookers, making my entrance as I would live my life—dramatically, on the leading edge, demonstrating a "new" way which is really not new at all but a reawakening of that which is simple, ancient, and completely natural.

There is an irony to this story which casts its long symbolic shadow into my life. One person not present in the room at my birth was my father. Hospital procedure dictated that expectant fathers were not allowed in the delivery room, so while I was surrounded by a group of interested strangers, my father had to remain in the waiting room. Neither my mother nor I was able to receive the support of the one person we most needed.

I was born on September 30, 1948, at 9:10 P.M.

The birth was smooth and successful. I arrived bright and alert and vocalizing loudly. Apparently I already had a lot to say.

MOTHER AND FATHER

My father's father came on a boat from Poland to America when he was sixteen years old. He was a brilliant man with a third-grade education, the black sheep of his family, and a rebel in the Catholic church in which he'd been raised. Like most immigrants he came to seek his fortune in the land of opportunity, but the extent of the fortune he found was to become a coal miner in a small town in Pennsylvania. When he was twenty-one he fell in love with, and married, a beautiful and headstrong Polish girl only fourteen years old. She was the oldest of eleven children and anxious to leave home. She gave birth to my father when she was fifteen, and later had two other sons. My grandfather's dream was that his sons would receive the education he never did. His sons exceeded his expectations: my father received his doctorate in engineering from the Massachusetts Institute of Technology, and both of his brothers eventually received their doctoral degrees. Shortly after I was born, my grandfather was killed in the coal mines.

On my mother's side, my family sailed from England to America on the second voyage of the Mayflower. They belonged to the Society of Friends (more commonly known as Quakers) and came seeking the freedom to practice their religion. I am descended from Benjamin Franklin's brother; Ben was my great-great-great-great-great-great-uncle!

The Quakers believe in living a simple life devoted to God and respecting and serving one's fellow beings. They are pacifists who refuse to serve in any war. They did not believe in slavery and helped many slaves escape to freedom in pre-Civil War and Civil War days. In the Friends' religion there is no minister to serve as intermediary between God and man. They believe and practice the truth that the spirit of God lives in all beings. For worship, the community gathers in a Sunday morning meeting where everyone sits in silent meditation until the spirit moves someone to speak. Friends used what they called the "plain language" in which they address one another as "thee" rather than "you"—a tradition intended to honor the presence of god within the person one is addressing. The plain language was used in my family up to my mother's generation. When my grandmother was alive I always slipped automatically into addressing her as "thee," and she of course always said "thee" to everyone in the family. One of my mother's favorite stories is about me at three years old, toddling up the hall to my grandmother's room at breakfast time to inquire, "Grandmother, is thee ready for thy egg?"

I feel the Quaker spirit has deeply influenced my life and my work, although it has taken me many years to consciously realize this. At times I have the experience of sitting with a group of people in one of my workshops or retreats and almost feeling my Quaker forefathers and mothers around me; I realize I am carrying on the tradition of recognizing the god within each person and creating the appropriate environments for that god spirit to come forth. Through my mother's family I received a deep imprinting of basic values and an attraction to a simple, natural lifestyle, as well as a desire and even a sense of obligation to serve humanity.

My grandmother and her siblings were the last generation to actively practice the Quaker religion. Grandmother married a non-Quaker man and moved to a small town in Texas where my mother and her brother were born and raised in a fairly typical small-town southern American environment. My grandparents' marriage was not a happy one, and my mother says that her parents would often go for days at a time barely speaking to each other, the house filled with the tension of unspoken hurt and resentment. During the depth of the Great Depression, when my mother was thirteen, her father, apparently despairing of being able to adequately support his family, simply abandoned them and disappeared. My grandmother worked and received some financial help from relatives, but even so, as with so many people in those times, there was not always enough to eat.

My mother was a very intelligent and aggressive child and her mother, a gentle soul, was always somewhat at a loss about how to handle her rather unruly daughter. My grandmother had a desire for her daughter to be dainty and feminine and my mother just didn't fit the picture. Also, my mother was quite psychic and sensitive, and she picked up and acted out the underlying anger and pain in the family. She played the role of the family scapegoat and rebel.

She graduated from high school and went away to college at the age of sixteen, relieved to leave the difficulties of her family and the restrictions of her social environment. Adventurous and willing to take risks, she set out to explore the world.

My great-great-grandmother had been a close friend and sister suffragette of Susan B. Anthony, and part of a strong family lineage of powerful, outspoken women who refused to play the traditional female role. My grandmother was an exception to this family heritage, but a couple of her sisters carried that energy and, of course, so did my mother. She saw herself as strong, capable of doing anything she wanted to do. And in fact, she became one of the first women city planners in the world, had a distinguished twenty-five-year career in that field, and has consistently lived her life on the leading edge.

My mother and father met in Boston during the war, where he was finishing his doctorate and she was working as a draftswoman in a radar lab. My father was brilliant and handsome, a talented classical pianist, fascinated with philosophy and science, and very scholarly. My mother was beautiful and sensuous, smart and powerful.

I recently saw an old home movie of the two of them having a picnic with some friends in a park during the early days of their relationship. It made me cry because they looked so young and beautiful, so happy and in love. I'm glad I have that picture of them in my heart, because things were never smooth for them. They had a difficult relationship from the beginning and decided to marry only after much ambivalence and deliberation. They were married just four years, and in a sense perhaps came together mainly to create me.

My father was still very much the dutiful son to his strong-willed mother. My mother, who was pretty strong-willed herself, resented this and was frustrated by his relative timidity about life. He was indecisive and unable to take a strong stand. She, on the other hand, was working through her own deep hurt and rage about the abandonment by her father and her feelings of being unloved as a child, and vented many of these feelings on my father. In recent times I've heard both of their descriptions of the relationship. I feel great sadness because I can see how frustrating and painful a mirror their relationship was for each of them.

I think they both wanted me, and hoped that the birth of a baby would help resolve some of their problems.

They were caring and loving parents to me as a baby. I had bad colic as an infant and apparently screamed loud and long. It must have been very trying, especially to my mother who was home with me while my father worked. My sense is that my stomach was upset by feeling the emotional pain of my parents. (I still have the same physical reaction when I am caught in a situation in which people are holding in unresolved painful feelings.)

My father recently told me the hardest thing he ever did in his life was to make the decision to leave me, and to separate from my mother. He cried when he told me that, and so did I.

He had to break a deep bond with me in order to feel free to leave what felt like an unbearable situation. Although I have no real memory of it at this time, I believe that the breaking of this bond with my father, and the subsequent feeling of emotional abandonment, was the most devastating experience of my life.

CHILDHOOD

My mother and father separated when I was a year-and-a-half old. For a year or so they lived near each other and I still saw my father regularly. Then they decided to divorce. My mother decided to go to St. Thomas in the Virgin Islands; if you spent six weeks there you could get an easy divorce. Meanwhile, she could have a vacation and heal some of her emotional wounds. So off she and I went to the Virgin Islands.

I didn't see my father again for a long time. My mother says that I showed no obvious emotional upset about the separation from my father. Perhaps at age two-and-a-half I was already coping with painful feelings by being strong.

At that time St. Thomas was truly a tropical paradise with very little development. My earliest memories are there. I remember playing in the sand by the blue sea. I remember a very large black woman named Seena who was my babysitter and whom I adored. And best of all, I remember the calypso music and dancing, bursting with primal energy. I first learned to dance to that music.

I had begun talking at an early age—about nine months. In St. Thomas I quickly picked up the "calypso" accent of the local people and began speaking that way. I learned to sing some of the popular calypso songs, and I still love to sing those songs. All in all, the beautiful black people of this island left a deep imprint on me through their music, dance, and speech, for which I am very grateful.

I have always been an "island" person. I love islands and feel most at home when I am on one. Most of the magic that I have found in my life has been on special islands.

My mother had come to St. Thomas intending to stay only for the six weeks necessary to get the divorce. However, she became so entranced with the place that we ended up staying a full year. In addition to enjoying the natural healing beauty of the island, she was having fun. Since it was inexpensive to live there, we had a beautiful house, and she had Seena to help with me. We went to the beach every day, she went dancing at night, and she met lots of interesting people. This was during the Korean War, and St. Thomas was a major "R & R" base for military personnel. There were dozens of ships making stops and lots of Navy, Marine, and Air Force men in circulation. All of them were eager for the company of an attractive woman, and my mother had a lot of dates, sometimes as many as four a day—one for lunch, one to go to the beach, one for dinner, and one for late-night dancing. I'm sure it was just what the doctor ordered after the pain of the divorce. Many of these men were lonely for their wives and children back home and were delighted to have contact with a three-year-old girl, so I received lots of attention too.

My mother tells the following story: For a while we stayed in a little cottage on the grounds of a hotel. I came down with the chicken pox, but it was a light case and I didn't feel very sick. However, since it was contagious she kept me isolated from other children. One day I was playing in the yard while she was gardening, and after a few minutes she noticed I had disappeared. She went searching for me and eventually found me in the hotel bar, sitting on a bar stool, chatting with a whole line of sailors who were buying me sodas, etc. She took me home, but a couple of hours later I disappeared again. She knew right where to go, and this time she found me entertaining a bunch of Marines. She later received a letter from a young officer she had dated that night, mentioning a sudden outbreak of chicken pox on his ship.

MOVING ON

When we finally left St. Thomas, it was hard for me to grasp the fact that we were no longer living on an island. I still wanted to go to the beach everyday, and I had a habit of making comments like, "This is the best store on the island," as if every town was on an island.

We went to live for a year or so in Texas, where my mother's family (my grandmother, uncle, and cousins) lived. Then we went to Mexico and settled in the town of San Miguel de Allende. Since it was inexpensive to live in Mexico, my mother figured she could live on my father's very moderate child support payments, not have to work, and try her hand at doing some writing. For a pittance we were able to rent a nice house with a courtyard, and hire a full-time cook named Luz (which means "light") and a part-time maid.

I was five years old when my mom enrolled me in a kinder-garten class. No one in the class spoke any English, including the teacher, so I had to pick up Spanish very quickly, which I did. Very soon I could converse in Spanish and was frequently called upon to translate for my mother when she spoke to the maid or went shopping. I even learned to make jokes and puns in Spanish. Our cook used to come to work at our house at dawn and I would say to my mother, "Mama, esta la manana, la Luz esta aqui!" (Mama, it's morning, the light—and/or Luz the cook—is here!)

There was an art college in San Miguel which attracted American art students and my mother soon found a crowd of intellectual, artistic friends. Once again she was living in an exotic place and having a good time, but she didn't get much writing done.

After we'd been in Mexico only a few months, my mother came down with hepatitis and became very ill. She needed constant care and there was really no one to provide it, so she arranged with a friend to drive us back to Texas where we lived with my grandmother for a few months while my mother recuperated. There has been very little illness in my family and this is about the only time I have ever seen my mother really sick. It was strange for me to see my normally strong mother so weak that I had to help her get up to go to the bathroom.

Once my mother was well we headed for California, where she had always dreamed of living. She needed to work to support us, and began to pursue her career as a city planner. When we first moved to California we lived in the San Francisco Bay area. Later, she became City Planner for the town of Tracy, then County Planning Director for Santa Cruz County, and eventually she worked for the state government in Sacramento. We moved every two or three years until I was in high school.

I liked the regular moving. The Tarot card that is connected with my birthdate is the Number Seven card—the Chariot— which relates to the principle of change and motion. Maybe this is why I was so well-suited to our gypsy lifestyle. I can remember as a kid thinking, "Well, we've been here for a couple of years now, I'm ready to go somewhere new." Possibly in part because we did move so often, and I felt a little outside of things anyhow, I often felt a bit different from other kids, so moving on was some- times a relief from a situation that wasn't comfortable for me anyway. And I always looked forward to the excitement of some- thing new.

I now feel that another part of me probably longed for more stability and continuity, but I was not at all in touch with that at the time. In fact, I am just beginning to know and acknowledge that part of myself, since it was strongly repressed by the circum- stances of my childhood.

I have the feeling that when my father left us, my mother and I formed an unconscious emotional pact that we would be strong for each other and take care of one another. She took care of my physical needs and taught me to be strong in dealing with the world. However, I sensed her underlying pain and unhappiness, and tried to take care of her emotionally. I remember at a young age feeling that I didn't want to tell her about any problems I was having which might add to her burden.

My mother never treated me much like a child. I was more like her traveling companion through the adventure of life. She respected me as an individual and treated me with a certain equality.

I responded by developing a mature, grown-up attitude. In the first few years of my life I spent much more time with my mother's adult friends than with other children, and I never developed any feelings of awe for adults or even any sense of being much different from them. In later childhood and adolescence this caused me some difficulties, since I was not at all intimidated by adults and had little sense of respect for their authority just because they were older than I was. I still have difficulty, sometimes, yielding to any type of authority other than the natural respect I give to someone who I feel genuinely knows more than I do in a given situation.

The positive aspect of my upbringing was that I developed strength and confidence in my ability to do things successfully in the world. The loss was that I never got to feel like a child. I was carrying a load of responsibility and I took it very seriously. I repressed my vulnerable feelings as well as much of the natural playfulness and lightness of childhood.

FATHER

In the three years between living in New Jersey and California I had seen my father only once—when he came to visit me in Texas when I was four. My mother didn't tell me he was coming because she was afraid he wouldn't show up and didn't want to risk my disappointment, so when he arrived at our door I was not expecting him. Because I had not seen him since I was two, she didn't know if I would recognize him. Apparently I looked up immediately and said, "Is that my daddy?" Though we were happily reunited and had a good visit, I didn't see him again until I arrived in California at age five-and-a-half. He had moved to California, too, so we began to have frequent contact. From then on he came to see me regularly, or I sometimes went to visit him. He was always very kind and loving to me, but a little emotionally removed, as if he felt he'd given up his right to really parent me by the fact of having left me. I always longed for more contact of some sort, but I didn't know exactly what I wanted, much less how to get it.

When I was six he married my stepmother, Babs, to whom he is still married. She had two sons from a previous marriage, Bruce and Scott, who became my stepbrothers (one and two years older than I), so when I visited my father I had a whole family to relate to. I liked my stepmother very much and felt comfortable with her. She is a beautiful, vivacious woman who is warm, intuitive, and motherly in a nice way. She's also bright and intelligent and I've always been able to talk to her about my life and ideas and concerns.

It was kind of exciting to have stepbrothers, since I'd never been around boys all that much. It was a bit traumatic sometimes as well. I can remember them teasing me until I cried, and I can also remember them making me laugh so much at dinnertime that I spit my food on the table and our parents sent all of us to our rooms. All this was very different from what I was used to—the relatively quiet home environment of just my mother and myself. I liked my "other" family, but it scared me a little, too. Again, I never felt completely a part of it, always a little outside. When I was eleven my father and stepmother had a daughter—Marianne. I liked playing with my little half-sister when I went for visits.

My father taught aeronautical engineering in graduate school. He is a true "absent-minded professor." I've seen him many times lapse into long silences as he stares into space, wrestling with some abstract mathematical problem. He is a wonderful teacher, loved and respected by his students, and enjoys talking about philosophy or politics or anything else of significance. He is almost totally uninterested in anything having to do with the material world and would be very happy if someone else simply made all the decisions relating to physical reality. In essence, he's a scholar, perhaps even a mystic by nature, although I don't think he'd be very comfortable with that term since he is decidedly nonreligious.

My mother, who had experienced profound spiritual feelings as a child, had also rejected any type of conventional religious beliefs by the time she was an adult. So I was raised in an atmosphere of intellectual rationalism and, throughout my childhood and adolescence, definitely considered myself an atheist. I thought that God was an idea people made up to make themselves feel better about the fact that they really didn't understand the origin, meaning, or ultimate outcome of life. I felt more comfortable simply admitting that I didn't have any answers to those questions. I still have a very strong rational voice which doesn't allow me to accept any ideas or beliefs unless I find some proof of their validity, or unless they resonate deeply with my strong inner sense of truth.

My view of my parents from my present perspective is that they are both profoundly mystical beings who, at the time, were cut off from any direct exploration of spirituality. My mother has since opened to the same types of consciousness pursuits that I have. My father continues to explore the mysteries of the universe primarily through philosophy and science.

Both my parents had a liberal political orientation, and politics were discussed frequently and ardently in both my mother's and father's households. I had a strongly developed social consciousness, a basic grasp of current political activities, and very adamant beliefs about it all from the time I was pretty young through my late teens.

LIFE WITH MOTHER

My childhood proceeded along its rather unconventional lines. My mother was extremely involved in her career and worked long hours — sometimes having meetings at night in addition to a full forty-hour work week. She always had interesting friends around, most of whom I liked and related to very well. My mother was responsible and practical, but often had a somewhat offbeat perspective on things. She enjoyed living on the edge of unconventional lifestyles and new ideas. One of her "beatnik" friends once described her this way, "Beth is popcorn, but she swings!" In more modern-day terminology that's somewhat equivalent to, "Beth is straight, but she's hip!"

She often did unusual, adventurous things that made life a

little more interesting. For example, when microwave ovens first came out, she bought one. In those days they were big, like a regular built-in oven. And rather than it being an addition to our kitchen, it was the only thing we had to cook with—we had no stove or regular oven. So I grew up cooking with a microwave at a time when no one else had even heard of one. When I left home I had to learn to cook all over again on a conventional stove.

Mom had an incisive mind and very strong opinions about things. Most of the time I agreed with her opinions, but when I didn't it was pretty pointless to try to change her mind. That didn't stop me from trying, though, and as I got older we sometimes had vehement arguments.

We traveled a lot whenever Mom had vacation time. We frequently drove across country to visit relatives or friends and to see the sights. When I was eight we took a really magical trip, sailing to Hawaii on a cruise ship, the Lurline. We spent a whole month in Hawaii. I was thrilled to be back on a tropical island, and spent hours playing in the ocean, pretending I was a mermaid. I also learned to dance the hula, which I loved.

When I was eleven we spent three weeks traveling around Europe, including several fascinating days in Russia, which was almost unheard-of in those Cold War times. Our trip was exciting, and I especially loved Italy. My most vivid memories are of an overnight train ride across the mountains from Austria into Italy, and later a train ride through the Swiss Alps which looked exactly as I had imagined from the book *Heidi*.

SCHOOL

I loved school and was a bright student. Schoolwork was easy for me, and I got a lot of praise and approval from my family and teachers for doing well. Most of my teachers liked me and gave me special attention; I think my enthusiasm and eagerness as a student stimulated them and made them feel appreciated.

Some of my teachers reacted to me in a very different way,

however. I can vividly remember having an argument with my third-grade teacher about the proper pronunciation of a word. When the dictionary proved me to be correct, she declared that the dictionary was wrong!

I had a year-long conflict with my sixth-grade teacher who seemed to resent me for reasons I never did really understand. In the eighth grade, the teacher threw me out of math class because I argued vehemently with him about the fact that he had marked every student's test paper down for one problem in which we all actually had the correct answer and he had the wrong one! I was sent to the counselor's office, where I explained the whole situation to her. She looked at the problem and acknowledged that I was correct, advised me to try to let it go, and managed to have me reinstated in class.

I suppose I must have seemed pretty obnoxious at times, but in my own mind I felt I was simply standing up for truth and justice and wasn't willing to cover up and pretend I didn't see what was happening. My mother cautioned me that I was going to have to learn to play by other people's rules a little bit more to avoid a lot of conflict in life, but I think it was already too late. I wasn't really a rebel. I simply refused to defer to authority when I thought it was wrong, and I was willing to fight for my point of view.

FRIENDS AND INTERESTS

Because I was an only child and my mother worked, I spent a lot of time alone and was used to creating my own activities. As a young child I had an active fantasy life, including an imaginary friend named Glunar, who was a constant companion. Glunar could be anything—a friend, a sister, a daughter—depending on what the game of the moment demanded. I remember wishing I could have an identical twin sister so that I would have a companion who would understand me perfectly and with whom I could share everything. At times I longed for an older brother, kind of a father substitute I suppose.

I must have been lonely, although I didn't think about it that way. When I was about ten, one of my friends mentioned to me that her mother thought I was lonely and needed someone. That remark really hurt my feelings and stuck in my mind for a long time.

Unlike almost everyone else in my generation, I had no television when I was a child. I occasionally watched TV at a friend's house, but for the most part I missed all the television lore so common to the experience of most of my peers. My mother chose not to have a television because she didn't want me to fall into the habit of sitting in front of the tube instead of developing my own interests. I can't say I regret it. To this day I don't like television much, and sometimes feel rather ill if I watch it more than a few minutes. It seems to have a numbing effect on my mind and body which I don't enjoy.

As a child, I was a total bookworm. I passionately loved books and was always reading one or more. The library was one of my favorite places. I went once or twice a week, spent hours poring over the various possibilities, and always checked out several which I then read voraciously. My mother would usually read to me before I went to sleep at night, a favorite ritual for both of us. I loved it when she would get really engrossed in the story and I could easily convince her to keep reading well past my bedtime.

When I was very young, some of my favorite books were the Mary Poppins books by P.L. Travers (there are several of them), *The Secret Garden*, and other classic books with a touch of magic.

Later on I got heavily into animal books, especially horse books like *The Black Stallion* and all of Walter Farley's other books, *Black Beauty*, and Marguerite Henry's books, including my all-time favorite, *King of the Wind*. Then I read some of the classics like *Jane Eyre* and *Wuthering Heights*, and a lot of historical fiction. (I remember staying up all night, utterly spellbound by *The Robe*.) One favorite was a romantic book about a half-Indian girl in early California, *Ramona*. I also read many of the books my mother had around. I always loved humorous books— some of my favorites were *Cheaper by the Dozen*, by Frank Bunker Gilbreth, *Auntie Mame*, by Patrick Dennis, and *Please Don't Eat the Daisies*, by Jean Kerr. I read each of those at least a dozen times.

I loved to write, too. I wrote poems and stories, and by the time I was eight or nine I was writing books. The books usually had many chapters, but I don't think I ever actually completed one. Most of my books were about a girl and her horse(s), although I later branched into more romantic themes involving girls and boys. I particularly remember one about a teenage girl who gets shipwrecked on a desert island with six young men! I think it's been lost but I wish I still had it because it sounds like a great fantasy.

Some of my later stories had magical or mystical overtones, such as the story of the rather conservative young man who keeps encountering a dark mysterious girl, who appears and disappears magically in his backyard.

I definitely wanted to be a writer when I grew up, and I used to visualize a shelf in the library filled with books I had written. Of course, I thought they would be fiction and would never have believed those books would turn out to be on metaphysical themes.

Interestingly enough, I stopped reading and writing when I was in high school and forgot all about my intention to be a writer. It was only after *Creative Visualization* was published years later that I remembered my early ambition and realized my childhood visualization had in fact manifested in form.

Like most children, I also did a lot of drawing. During my horse phase I got pretty good at drawing horses, and what I liked best was drawing them in action, using relatively few lines to convey the beauty of their bodies and movements.

I used to imagine that I was going to have twelve children (influenced no doubt by my beloved book, *Cheaper by the Dozen*). I remember writing a list of the names I would give all my future children. Then I drew designs for a house with thirteen bedrooms for all of us to live in. After that I designed a barn with stalls for each of our horses (all the horses had, of course, been suitably named as well).

My greatest love was for animals, and animals were my dearest companions. When I was an infant, the first word I spoke was the name of our cocker spaniel—Muff—and I took my first step toward her. Throughout childhood I always had birds, fish, turtles, etc. The first cuddly pet of my own was a guinea pig named Spice, whom I loved dearly. It was a big thrill when, a few months after we brought her home from the pet store, she gave birth to four adorable babies.

I always longed for a dog, so on my eighth birthday my parents gave me a purebred German Shepherd puppy named Prince Valiant. He quickly grew up to be a big, gorgeous, energetic dog. Prince definitely brought a note of virile, male energy into our placid female household. He was always getting loose and chasing smaller dogs in the neighborhood, and when I took him for walks on a leash he usually dragged me wherever he wanted to go. When he wagged his big tail he swept everything off our coffee table! I was crazy about him, and he was the companion/protector/brother/friend that I needed.

Unfortunately, when we moved to Santa Cruz when I was eleven, we didn't have a yard for him. I gave him to a family who lived on a large ranch with acres for him to run on. He was probably happier, but I missed him. To help take the place of Prince, my father brought me a little female Siamese kitten I named Fa-ying, after a Siamese princess in the book, *Anna and the King of Siam*. Fa-ying became my beloved friend and was with me until I was twenty-one.

Of course, I always yearned desperately for a horse. I was particularly attracted to Arabian horses and fantasized about having one of my own. Not only did I read, write about, and draw horses constantly, but I acted like a horse most of the time. I never walked, skipped, or ran; I always jogged, trotted, and galloped, tossing my mane and neighing as I went, then stopping to paw the ground and snort. I never played with dolls much, but I had a set of toy horses that were totally alive to me—each with its own name and personality. I rode horses whenever I got the chance, and went every year to the annual Arabian horse show at the San Francisco Cow Palace. To my disappointment, I never got a horse of my own.

From a very young age I had a strong sense of responsibility.

I can remember at the age of eight getting up early in the morning and making my bed, waking my mother up, then carefully feeding and taking care of my birds, my tropical fish, my guinea pig, and my dog before getting dressed and going off to school.

Despite being an only child and moving frequently, I made friends fairly easily, and from the time I started school I always had neighborhood friends my own age to play with. For some inexplicable reason, the year I was in fourth grade I suddenly became the most popular girl in my class—other girls fought to hold my hand when we went out to play at recess. My arch rival was a very pretty, flirtatious girl named Nicole. While my girlfriends and I played horses at recess, she and her clique would turn cartwheels and somersaults, showing off their petticoats. I thought they were silly and disgusting. Nicole and I both liked the same boy—a young charmer named Allan who never let on which one of us he preferred, but managed to keep us both on the hook.

The following year Nicole moved away and my social position vanished as mysteriously as it had come. I still had friends but I was no longer the center of everyone's attention. No one fought to hold my hand anymore. I felt abandoned and betrayed. I never understood this whole experience and it left me with a vague insecurity about why, or whether, people really liked me.

MUSIC

My best friend in those times was a girl named Carol Jacobsen. She played the cello and her whole family was very musical. Her parents were good friends of my mother's and we used to spend many evenings at their house. There were always musicians there playing chamber music, so when I spent the night with Carol, I would fall asleep to the beautiful strains of live classical music floating in from the living room. I loved being a part of this warm home full of people and music.

I took piano lessons for about a year. My mother recently told me that when I first began, I used to practice for hours relentlessly, and end up in tears. Apparently I had the idea that I ought to be able to learn it *all* right away and was frustrated when I couldn't! Eventually I switched from piano to violin lessons.

I continued to study and play violin for ten years, and even played for a couple of years in the California Junior Symphony. I loved it, but when I went to college I got distracted by too many other things and stopped playing. One of my fantasies is that I will someday take it up again. I'd also like to play the electric violin, and the electric guitar!

About the time I started playing violin and became interested in classical music, rock 'n roll was just beginning to blast through the repressed consciousness of the late fifties. I remember hearing the wild beat on transistor radios kids brought to school, and hearing them talk excitedly about the latest hits. I was firmly entrenched in my precocious concept of myself as a young intellectual and considered myself above it all—rock 'n roll was the music of the rabble as far as I was concerned.

By the time we moved to Santa Cruz when I was in sixth grade, though, I began to get interested. Adolescence was beginning to stir up my hormones and rock 'n roll seduced me. By the seventh grade I was a full-fledged addict.

Robin Simpson became my best friend; I used to go over to her house after school and on weekends. I'd spend the night there and we'd listen to the radio or records, talk endlessly about life and boys, and fantasize about the possibility of meeting Elvis.

I was completely in love with Elvis. I resisted him at first, and then fell head over heels. His sensuous voice—singing or speaking—his charm, his wild rebellious maleness combined with a certain feminine sensuality just devastated me. I still have the original records of a lot of his early music and they are still some of my all-time favorite listening. I believe he was a very powerful channel.

In the fifties, it seemed as though white western culture was close to extinction from sheer repression of its emotional, instinctual, sexual energy. Our juices weren't flowing and we were in danger of drying up and blowing away. Thank God that the life force was being preserved and nurtured by the black culture in our midst. Though our ignorant and savage American forefathers had gone to Africa for the basest of objectives—slavery—they brought back black people still in touch with the earth and with themselves, to eventually save us. Of course, white people could not deal with this confrontation with their shadow selves which they so desperately needed, and for generations they busily built walls of prejudice and segregation to keep themselves safe from the threatening presence of so much vitality and aliveness.

Salvation had to come through music, and come it did. And it had to reach us through a white man because the white culture wouldn't accept a black man or God forbid, a black woman! So Elvis got his giant soul born into a white body and let it come through him. Of course there were lots of others, black and white, who were just as important in this process. But he was the figurehead, the symbol, and the first major channel through which rock 'n roll blasted us alive.

I don't think it's any accident that so many people still adore him, and worship him almost like a god. I feel he was a very powerful entity who served us all, and like so many others with power, he didn't know how to handle it, he didn't understand it, and it destroyed him most tragically.

I went through a similar infatuation a few years later with the Beatles. I fell in love with John Lennon—another great channel who I feel was demolished by his power. There have been so many in the world of rock 'n roll, and I thank them all for their gifts and their willingness to play out our repressed dark sides, the shadow sides of our civilized personalities which we try to ignore but without which we cannot live.

LOOKING FOR LOVE

My mother never married again, although she came close a couple of times. She had a number of significant relationships, and even became engaged once, but in the end decided against the marriage. In my early childhood, several of these men made a strong connection with me and played an important father role. I felt loved by them, and adored them in return. Unfortunately, when their relationship with my mother dissolved for one reason or another, I never saw them again. So the pattern of feeling loved by a father and then unexpectedly abandoned was thoroughly reinforced.

Since I had no brother or grandfather and my only uncle lived in Texas, there was a definite shortage of male energy in my life. As a result, I was curious and fascinated by the mysterious male of the species, very attracted to them, and desirous of their love and attention.

As far back as I can recall, I've always been in love. I remember as vividly as if it were yesterday at age five going with my mother to a Christmas party at her boss's house and meeting his son who was my age. It was love at first sight, and we walked around the rest of the evening holding hands. I was thrilled, and it felt very natural. Throughout grade school I always had a crush on some boy in my class. I'm sure the feelings were often mutual, but they were not usually openly acknowledged or acted on.

The summer of my eleventh year I went to 4-H camp and fell in love with an "older man" of fourteen—Carl. He joked around with me and paid me some attention but that was the extent of our interaction. I loved him passionately for the entire next year. I was crushed when I went back to camp the following year with high hopes, only to find him in a heavy romance with a very sexy-looking girl his own age named Judith (I hated her!).

The next summer I fell in love with a second cousin at a family gathering and spent the next year pining unrequitedly for him. I started going out occasionally with boys, and received my first real kiss from an otherwise pretty unremarkable young man.

I was fourteen, we had moved to Sacramento, and I was in the ninth grade when my first real romance struck like a bolt out of the blue. I was playing violin in the California Junior Symphony—one of the newest and least accomplished members, seated way back in the second violin section.

The first violinist and star of the symphony was a tall, blonde nineteen-year-old young god named Robin. We were performing a symphony in which he played a very dramatic and difficult solo, and I was totally in awe of him. Through an odd fluke, my mother started dating his father and they arranged for me to take violin lessons from Robin.

Midway through my first lesson my knees were weak and I definitely could not concentrate on the music. He apparently felt the same way and our violin lessons soon transformed into passionate kisses and earnest discussions about life. We went out together for a few weeks. He took me to some parties with his intellectual existentialist friends who seemed quite amused to meet me. While I was intellectually precocious, I was basically a naive fourteen-year-old while he was a sophisticated nineteen. I was in romantic bliss, but had no idea what he saw in me. Whatever it was, he apparently thought better of it, because he suddenly stopped coming over or calling. I was too shy to call him. The symphony season ended and I no longer saw him.

The pattern of love and abandonment was already surfacing in this new arena of romance. The effect was devastating and I crashed into a semisuicidal depression. My intense emotional pain was entwined with my new-found existential philosophy and I began to question the very meaning of life. I found none. I fell into complete despair and hopelessness. For the first time, I lost interest in school; I sat in class and stared into space, or moped morosely around the house. My mother was so concerned about me that she sent me to a therapist, who put me in a group with other troubled teenagers. I found that interesting, and it probably helped some, but the depression continued for several months and recurred periodically for the next few years. I never really regained my motivation for excelling in school. I continued to make good grades because it was pretty easy for me to do so, but I didn't put out the effort to do as well as I might have.

I'm sure part of this was due to the usual adolescent blues, and part of it came from the surfacing of unresolved pain from my childhood (which may be what the adolescent blues is really all about for most people).

On another level I was undergoing a spiritual crisis. My emotional despair was forcing me to confront the underlying emptiness of the life I was living—a life focused on intellectual and external pursuits but with little connection to the greater spirit. Without that inner spiritual connection, life feels meaningless, and we try to run away from facing that feeling by pursuing even harder the things we hope will provide us with satisfaction. I was already beginning to see that the things I had thought significant were not in themselves going to bring me fulfillment. Relationships, success, the admiration of others, money, education, even creative endeavors or service to others, while wonderful in themselves, were not enough to give my life true meaning and purpose. At that time I had no idea what was missing; I just knew that if this was all there was to life, I didn't want to go on living.

Although I distracted myself as much as I could, this despair lingered close to the surface for the next several years, pulling me toward a new level of opening.

I now know that everyone, sooner or later, in one way or another, must face this crisis. In eastern philosophy it is called "piercing the veil of illusion." We must see beyond our focus on the world of form in order to open to the fullness of the world of spirit. As we make that transition we experience ourselves moving into total darkness—the darkness of our own fear that there is nothing beyond what we know with our physical senses. In facing the depth of our own fear, we finally allow ourselves to encounter directly the power, beauty, and love of the great spirit that is alive in all of creation.

ADOLESCENCE

I had always been tall for my age (at twelve I was nearly my present height of five feet, nine inches), and for years had towered over most of the boys my age. So I was delighted when I started high school (in Sacramento, high school started in tenth grade) and noticed that over the summer the kids my age seemed to have grown remarkably. Also, there were now lots of older kids, so the halls were filled with tall boys!

My broken heart was finally healed when I started going with Rick, a bright, interesting boy my own age whom I had always liked. This was my first long-lasting, reciprocated romance. We shared much in common and really loved each other. We were fifteen, still too young to drive (a source of unbearable frustration—we yearned for the ultimate symbol of independence, the driver's license), so we had to ride bikes to each other's houses and walk to movies, or (God forbid) even get rides from our parents. His parents sensed the depth of our connection and were very concerned that we might get overly emotionally and/or sexually involved. We did a lot of passionate necking, but in those days it was still pretty unusual to have sex at that age, and we didn't. We broke up at the end of that school year because we were just too young to sustain the intensity of our connection. The next year I went with a very sweet guy from the local junior college who ended up marrying one of my best girlfriends after he and I broke up.

My girlfriends were at least as important as my boyfriends, if not more so. I formed deep friendships with four other girls—Yvonne, Bev, Sandy, and Cathy—and the five of us made quite a formidable team. We spent most of our time together and shared everything. On weekends we often would spend the night at one of our houses, talking late into the night and laughing so hard and long our stomachs ached. Sometimes we did crazy things like sneak out in the middle of the night after we were supposed to be asleep and dance wildly around in the park like Dionysian-worshipping nymphs. We talked endlessly, of course, about our boyfriends and everything we were learning and experiencing with them. We also talked about everything else, especially about the meaning of life and how we thought our lives would take shape. They were really special young women and I look back on our time together with passionate fondness. Sandy, who later changed her name to Sonora, remained my best friend until we were thirty.

There were a couple of favorite teachers who very much influenced my life at that time. One was Mr. Lahey, my counselor and English teacher, who recognized my intelligence and creativity and gave me support at a time when I really needed it. He told me I had a "facile pen" (meaning I wrote easily and well) and encouraged me to express myself in writing. He was a devout Catholic, and one day when I was feeling really troubled and depressed he told me he felt that I needed to find God. At the time I was disgusted by what I felt to be ridiculous advice, but many times since I have thought back on the essential truth of his comment. I wish I could let him know how right he was.

Another favorite of mine was Mr. Gill, my Latin teacher. I studied Latin during all three years of high school, so I was in his class every year. He was a large, red-haired young Irish-American who had studied for the priesthood, and then decided to get married and became a high school teacher. We could tell he really loved kids, and he was a lot of fun. We got Latin out of the way as quickly as possible and spent most of our time in class talking about current events and arguing over politics and philosophy.

This was 1963-66, just as the Vietnam war was escalating and heating up as a controversial topic. I held strong antiwar sentiments and participated in demonstrations and wrote letters to the editor of the city newspaper. Mr. Gill thought the war was right and necessary, so he and I had daily heated arguments in which some of the other kids participated, while others probably wondered if we'd lost our minds and waited impatiently for the bell to ring. I loved his class and was grateful that he provided a forum for talking about meaningful things and encouraged us to speak out about our feelings and opinions. When I applied to college I asked him to write a letter of recommendation for me. I was astounded when I later found out he had written that he expected me to be "one of the great women of this century." Tears come to my eyes right now as I write this. Thank you for appreciating me, Mr. Gill.

When I turned seventeen at the beginning of my senior year, I decided it was time to lose my virginity. One of my girlfriends had already made the leap and I didn't want to get left too far behind. I had started going out with a young man of nineteen who was in the Navy, and stationed nearby. Jim was smart, fun, and rebellious (he hated the Navy), and he cared about me. He seemed like a good candidate to help me achieve my goal.

My mother had decided, rather belatedly, that I needed to have a little more structure and enforced a rigid curfew—I had to be in by midnight no matter what, even on weekends. So I engaged in my first major rebellion. I would come in at midnight, go to bed, then after my mother was asleep I'd sneak out my window and Jim would pick me up in his car. Of course by that hour there was nowhere to go, so we'd cruise around in the car and end up parking and making out. So that was the scene for my first sexual experience—the back seat of a car. Like most first experiences it was not particularly good, but I did kind of enjoy the daring rebelliousness of it all.

Jim and I continued to go together, and with a little practice the sex got better. Unfortunately, with typical young-girl naiveté, I managed to get pregnant within the first two months.

PREGNANCY

I was still dealing with my underlying existential despair and had begun questioning whether I even wanted to follow the life plan that I felt was practically mapped out for me—go to a good college, become a professional something, and pursue a meaningful career. When I got pregnant, I started fantasizing about not going to college at all but marrying Jim and becoming a housewife with a baby. The complete change from my programmed path appealed to me.

At this point my mother guessed I was pregnant and we had a long talk about it. She convinced me to think things through a little more, and in the end I decided I wasn't ready to have a child. At that time abortion was still illegal in the U.S. and conjured up horrible pictures of sinister doings in back rooms. Abortion was completely legal, however, in Sweden and Japan. My mother asked around for advice among her friends, and a Japanese friend offered to arrange for me to have a legal abortion in Japan through her sister who lived there. My mother and I decided it would be better for me to travel there and have a legal operation rather than risk an illegal situation here. The operation would cost almost nothing, but the trip would be expensive. My mother could afford to pay my way but not to accompany me.

Jim was upset because he wanted to marry me and have the child. I sensed, however, that part of his desire was based on his desperate need to have something warm and comforting to offset his miserable Navy life, and I really didn't want to carry that burden. So during the high school spring break I told everyone except my best girlfriends (they knew the real story) that I was going to visit a family in Japan, and off I went.

I was met in the Tokyo airport by our friend's sister, an elderly Japanese lady who spoke some English and took me to the small private hospital of a young Japanese obstetrician.

The doctor spoke no English. There was no heat in the place and it seemed a little primitive. The situation was so different from what I had imagined (I had pictured a large, white-washed institution) that I began to panic.

I excused myself and went to the bathroom. It had an Asian-style toilet on the floor that you squat over. Everything was so strange and foreign. The last straw was when I tried to leave the bathroom, and the door stuck and I couldn't get out. I pounded on the door and started crying hysterically. I felt I was going to die in this strange place, far from anything familiar or anyone who cared about me.

They rescued me from the bathroom and I immediately called my mother. She must have been extremely worried to hear me so upset, but she managed to sound very reassuring. I began to calm down; the doctor and my interpreter urged me to get a good night's sleep.

The next morning the doctor informed me there would be two operations, one in the morning and one in the evening. He gave me a general anesthetic and performed the first procedure. I was violently ill all day long. Then he did the second operation and I felt fine after that. To this day I have no idea why it was done that way.

I stayed in the hospital recuperating for several days, during which time I fell in love with my doctor and his family. They were extremely kind to me, probably feeling terribly sorry for this young American girl so far from home. His wife cooked for me, trying to make me American food though I would rather have eaten Japanese. His two little daughters visited me every day after school. And before I departed he invited me and my interpreter/caretaker to have tea with him and his aged parents who lived with him in a little rice-paper house next to the clinic. I'll never forget standing there feeling about eight feet tall and totally awkward as all the little Japanese people knelt and bowed their heads to the ground (politeness requires that you get lower than the other person). I deeply appreciated their kindness, and when I left my heart felt full to overflowing with love for them.

My mother had reasoned that as long as we were paying all this money for a trip to Japan, I might as well get some enjoyment and culture from it. She had arranged for me to go on a little three-day tour with some other Americans to the beautiful, historic city of Kyoto. Because of my readjusting hormones, I was on an emotional rollercoaster—euphoric one minute and depressed and lonely the next. It was strange not being able to talk to anybody about why I was really there. I loved Kyoto, however. The elegance and beauty of the temples and gardens resonated deep in my soul. It all seemed very familiar, and I felt I wanted to come there again.

On the way home from Japan, I stopped in Honolulu for a few days. Our travel agent had made a reservation for the least expensive room in a hotel right on Waikiki Beach, which in those days had only a few hotels and was still quite lovely and unspoiled. The cost of the room was only eight dollars a night! I arrived on Easter Sunday, the last day of Easter vacation. The hotel had been full, but as most people had checked out that morning and it was almost empty, the desk clerk gave me one of the best rooms in the hotel for the same price! It was on the top floor, had balconies looking out in two directions, a beautiful turquoise carpet the color of the sea outside, and a large gold bed. I was overwhelmed, but pleased.

My stay in Hawaii was healing to my body and psyche. The soft warm air and the sun on the beach felt like they penetrated every pore. I met a handsome twenty-four-year-old pool hustler from New York City named Eddie who must have sensed my vulnerability because he took me under his wing, showed me around, didn't try to get in the gold bed with me, and gave me a chastely romantic good-bye kiss when I left.

The overall impression of my trip was one of going forth into the world, alone and vulnerable, and being completely taken care of and treated with great kindness by everyone I encountered. It was a powerful experience of trusting myself and others. I knew I could never repay the people who had helped me, but I vowed to pass that same caring on to others in need.

COLLEGE

My mother's best friends, Tom and Delphine Frazier, who had been like an aunt and uncle to me, both had graduated from Reed College in Portland, Oregon. I had a long-standing ambition to go there, too. Not only did Reed have one of the highest academic standards in the country, but it was known to be a creative, radical, and unconventional environment long before the radicalism of the late 1960's erupted on all the college campuses. To my delight, my application was accepted; I went off to college in the fall of 1966.

Reed is a small (at that time about 900 students), private college located on a lush, green, spectacularly beautiful campus in residential Portland. My first year I lived in a wonderful old stone dormitory on campus. Reed was a very stimulating environment because everyone there—professors and students—was quite brilliant. Although very academically oriented, they de-emphasized grades and encouraged freedom of spirit and creative thinking and action. There were a lot of real characters there, on the staff and in the student body. My thirst for knowledge, somewhat dulled in high school, was re-awakened. I was thrilled to be beginning my adult life in such an exciting place.

It was traumatic for me as well. I had been accustomed all my life to receiving strokes for my intelligence. I was used to being one of the smartest people around and always easily excelled at anything I put my mind to. At Reed everyone was at least as smart as I was, and many of them seemed quite a bit smarter and better educated. Many students had gone to east coast private schools and had a certain sophisticated literariness that was completely over my head. I soon discovered that I couldn't just write a paper and automatically get an "A." I had to work at it, and even then it wasn't always great. My entire ego identity as a brilliant intellectual was severely shaken.

My college career started with an intense incident. As I mentioned, Reed was a hotbed of radical politics, and 1966 was a radical time. I immediately got involved in a campus anti-Vietnam war group and began to take an active part in demonstrations. One night there was a big, important one. Hubert Humphrey, who was then U.S. Vice President, was attending a fund-raising banquet in Portland with all the local bigwigs. We staged a demonstration out front which started peacefully, but began to get frightening when a long line of helmeted policemen appeared and began to descend menacingly upon us. A melee broke out and things became wild and chaotic. At one point a young man, a demonstrator, had fallen on the ground right in front of me and a burly policeman began kicking him viciously. I was carrying a picket sign and my reflex reaction was to bring it down on the officer's head. It was made of cardboard and he was wearing a helmet so he barely noticed it, but another policeman who witnessed it came up behind me, grabbed me, and started hauling me off toward the paddy wagon.

I guess I'm not really cut out to be a revolutionary heroine because I'm ashamed to say I completely lost my nerve and began babbling, "I didn't mean it, I didn't mean it!" (I really didn't intend to hit a policeman, it was kind of an involuntary reaction.) I'll never forget the officer's gruff reply as he threw me in the paddy wagon, "Yes you did, you little phoney!"

They hauled a bunch of us off to jail. When they discovered I was a few days under eighteen they took me to juvenile hall, which was really frightening because I was separated from my companions and kept there most of the night. All the attending officers and matrons were incredibly cold and unfeeling and that terrified me. I knew I would eventually be rescued, but I found myself thinking of what it must be like to be some poor minority kid in trouble without anyone to effectively defend you. A very desperate feeling.

About 3:00 A.M. my college dean came and got me out. He was a sweet man, and to me he looked like an angel. My mother later told me the juvenile hall matron had called her in California in the middle of the night and told her that her daughter had attacked a policeman, that he had been hospitalized, and they didn't know if he was going to be all right! My mother kept her composure, asked for details, and finally said, "Do you mean to tell me that a skinny seventeen-year-old girl hit a helmeted policeman with a cardboard picket sign and you don't know if he is going to be all right?"—at which point the policewoman hung up on her.

I was assured by knowledgeable friends that since I was under eighteen the arrest would not go on my record, which relieved me greatly. I never heard another word about the incident.

I soon adjusted to college life. My two roommates became close girlfriends, I had a nice boyfriend, and I liked my classes. For my physical education requirement, I enrolled in a ballet class. I had always loved ballet—even as a small child my mother took me to see performances of the San Francisco Ballet and I was always on the edge of my seat. I had fantasized about being a ballerina but had never pursued it, though I did take a modern dance class in high school which I really enjoyed. The teacher at Reed was very good and I loved the class. I began to get more and more involved, and took ballet classes as often as I could.

During my second year at Reed I began to be disillusioned with school. Reed intensified my tendency toward intellectualism to the maximum and I was becoming saturated. I remember feeling that I was spending ninety percent of my life in my head, and I was yearning for other parts of my being to be expressed, but there was little opportunity for that since I had to spend most of my time studying. I had decided to major in psychology, which really interested me, but the basic classes there were behaviorist-oriented and mostly had to do with experimenting with rats and compiling statistics, both of which I hated. My existential ennui was setting in again, in full force. Once more I was wondering what the point of it all was.

CHANGES

At this time there were three factors in my life which began to alter my consciousness and shift my perception of reality.

The first one was drugs. Marijuana and LSD were just coming into common usage on college campuses, and Reed was right on the forefront. Some of my friends had been using drugs but I was more cautious. I had never smoked a cigarette nor drunk much alcohol, and had hardly ever used so much as an aspirin. In my freshman year I had tried to smoke marijuana a couple of times, but since I didn't know how to smoke, nothing much happened.

In my second year I tried again and finally mastered the technique enough to get the effect, which turned out to be very pleasant. I began smoking it occasionally and enjoyed the way it helped me to see things from a different perspective.

Eventually I tried LSD a few times and had some wonderful experiences with it. It allowed me to feel very free and expanded, and to experience the physical world on the level of energy. I was able to see how everything physical is actually made of energy, and to tune into the vibration of that energy. Although my drug experiences were quite positive, I never developed the habit of using drugs more than occasionally, unlike some of my friends, who used them regularly. When it comes to food and substances I have a very nonaddictive personality. I seem to have a strong need for balance and health, and a natural inclination away from excess. Also, I come from a family of nondrinkers and nonsmokers. I even think the fact that I was not anesthetized when I was born may have helped free me from the tendency toward drug addiction so prevalent in my generation.

Toward the end of my second year, I had the second experience which was a major turning point in my life. I had formed a strong connection with a young psychology professor who invited me to participate in an experiment—an "encounter group" composed of a number of the Reed faculty and a few students. These types of groups were a new phenomenon and none of us had ever been to one before.

About twenty of us gathered in the living room of a house belonging to one of the professors. The group leader began by having us introduce ourselves and tell the others a little about some of the problems and issues we were dealing with in our lives. Then he had us do some exercises with partners, looking in each other's eyes, asking and answering certain questions. I began to feel many emotions—some sadness, some feelings of love. Other people were becoming emotional, too. Eventually some people started to cry, releasing intense feelings they had been holding back all their lives.

We spent three days together. During that time, everyone expressed more and more of their emotions. When people got angry, the leader would facilitate them in expressing their emotions. The more we shared, the closer we all felt to each other. By the end of the session, it was as if we were one big, intimate family.

I was in bliss. I had never felt such powerful feelings of love before. For days afterward I felt even higher than I had on drugs. My heart was wide open. I knew I wanted more of this feeling.

DANCE

The third major influence toward change at that time was dance. There was a new teacher that year who taught modern dance instead of ballet. I loved the feeling of freedom and power I got from moving my body in new ways. It provided the balance for my intellect that I needed so desperately, and I began to realize it was the only class I really enjoyed! By the end of the school year I had developed a serious interest in dance, so I decided to attend a six-week intensive dance summer school program held at Long Beach State College in California.

It was a fabulous experience for me. I lived in a dormitory

with other dance students and we took dance classes six hours a day, six days a week. The rest of the time we talked, ate, and breathed dance. There were top-notch teachers there and we studied ballet, many forms of modern dance, jazz, and choreography. I was completely excited about dancing, and I loved the focus, rigor, and discipline of the almost monastic life I was living.

When I went back to Reed to begin my third year, a strange thing happened. I walked into the office to register for the classes I wanted and suddenly realized that I couldn't do it. I simply turned around and walked out again.

In that moment of choice I turned my back on my old identity and the life I had been trained and programmed for since birth. I think it may have been the most radical leap I ever made.

DANCE AND DISCOVERY

Through dance I had my first experiences of letting go of control and surrendering fully into the energy of life. I released my mind and allowed the life force to dance me. I experienced the power of the universe moving through my body, sweeping me into ecstasy.

It changed my life forever. I could no longer return to my former rational existence. My old identity and my previous priorities had dissolved, and I had no idea who I was or where I was going.

I stayed in Portland that year, and rented a little house near the Reed campus with my current boyfriend, a rather mystical, very stoned young man whom I met in San Francisco and invited to Portland to live with me. I got a job teaching dance to children for the city recreational department, and also took dance classes at Reed. Thank God for my teacher, who sat down with me every week and told me what to teach the children in my class. I felt I was only one jump ahead of them and was very anxious about the whole thing. Apparently I did fine, because in the city-wide performance at the end of the year my kids were spectacular and I was very proud of all of us.

The year off from school allowed me time to integrate the changes I was going through and find my new direction.

I decided to follow my passion for dance. I reasoned I could only do that while I was young, whereas other things could be pursued later in life. I decided to complete my college education by getting my degree in dance. Since Reed didn't have a dance major, I transferred to the University of California at Irvine, which had a very strong dance department. It was quite a switch from Reed to Irvine, which is located in Orange County, a bastion of conservatism just south of Los Angeles. Irvine was the polar opposite of Reed, a large, brand new, and utterly bland campus for middle America. I ignored everything about it except my dance classes.

The Irvine dance department was competing for its reputation against the well-known dance department of UCLA. UCLA was known for turning out dancers who were creative choreographers or teachers but not professional performers. Irvine's department, under the direction of Eugene Loring, was determined to graduate students who were technically competent to become professional dancers. So the emphasis was on technique—ballet, modern, and jazz, with some choreography. Standards were very high, grading was extremely tough, and the competition was intense.

I was at a great disadvantage because I had only started dancing three years before, whereas most of the students had been studying ballet since childhood. I worked hard, enjoying the focus and discipline, and gained a solid technical foundation for which I am still grateful. The technical emphasis was good for me in that I needed the training, but the competitive atmosphere was stressful and discouraging. I loved choreography and began to have fantasies about a career as a choreographer. I later wished that I had received more support for the creative aspect of dance, in which I feel I could have excelled.

During my junior year at Irvine I didn't have a steady boyfriend, for the first time since I was fifteen. I lived in a house on Balboa Island with two other women, and focused almost completely on my dance studies.

At this time I developed an interest in health food and began cooking and eating very consciously. My girlfriend from high school, Sonora, had started practicing hatha yoga and told me about it. It sounded interesting, so I began taking a yoga class and practicing every day. I was devoting my life to developing a healthy, powerful relationship with my body. And being alone afforded me time for contemplation, which began to put me in touch with my deeper self. Again I had that monastic feeling, which I found very satisfying to my soul. I still think back on the relative simplicity and physical discipline of that time with a certain yearning.

On an emotional level I was pretty lonely, though. Not having a relationship with a man seemed to leave me with an empty, aching feeling inside. So by my second year at Irvine I fell in love with Laurence. We found a cute, funky little cottage way out in the country and moved in together. Laurence worked as a salesman for a carpet cleaning company. Since I needed a job that would fit around school we decided to start our own carpet cleaning company. I was the saleswoman who went out to give the estimates and make the sales, and Laurence did the actual cleaning. I discovered that I enjoyed the contact with people and had a certain knack for sales. It was mainly a matter of being warm and friendly to people and letting them know that I cared about them.

Our business flourished and we eventually moved back to town, got a large modern apartment with a room for our office, and hired a couple of phone solicitors to get the leads. ("Hi, this is Miraclean carpet cleaners. We are going to be in your area giving free estimates ... ") We weren't getting rich, but we were supporting ourselves. (Later, after I left, Laurence sold the business and apparently it is still flourishing.)

I had a vague interest in eastern philosophy, and had read an Alan Watts book or two. A wonderful old art history professor at

Reed, Dr. Reynolds, had a bent toward eastern mysticism and used to show us slides of oriental art and murmur things about the "cosmic void," which kind of fascinated me although I really didn't understand what he was talking about. He taught us that in order to appreciate art, we must sit in front of the painting or object and try to empty our mind of all thoughts, judgments, and interpretations, then simply open ourselves to receive whatever the work might be trying to communicate to us. I tried my best to practice what he suggested, although it was not easy because I was so used to being in my head. Dr. Reynolds also taught calligraphy; he asked us to write out our art history papers in longhand and graded us on the visual artistry as well as the content. I loved this, since I hate typing, and to this day I write everything in longhand.

Now that I was practicing yoga regularly, I became interested in the idea of meditation. Laurence also had an interest in spiritual growth, and we began reading some metaphysical books. The first one that had a major impact on me was *Autobiography of a Yogi*, by Paramahansa Yogananda. Though I was still very skeptical of anything nonrational, this book drew me in very powerfully with its descriptions of other realities. There was something about it that fascinated me and resonated deep within my own being. I met a couple of other people who were interested in these ideas and we used to sit around and discuss them for hours. Sometimes these discussions were enhanced by a few puffs on a joint, which really allowed us to get into cosmic realms of nonlinear reality.

I had shared my interest in yoga with my mother, who was now living in Washington, D.C., and working for the federal government. She became interested as well, took a yoga class, and started practicing yoga daily as a way to relax and to deal with a long-standing back problem. After a few months of yoga she had permanently healed her back (after fifteen years of chronic pain) and was more physically fit at age fifty than she had been in years.

In June of 1971 I graduated from college. Unfortunately, most of my initial passion for dance had been buried under discouragement. I had spent too much time competing to fit someone else's technical standards rather than developing the expression of my own unique creative spirit. I still feel sad and angry when I think of the unnecessary loss of my bright young inspiration and enthusiasm. I've heard so many others tell this same story about their formal education—especially in the arts. Technique is important, but needs to be kept in perspective. It is developed to serve the spirit, not squelch it!

I had no idea what to do next. I had a bachelor's degree in dance, but that in itself didn't do me much good. I felt uncertain in what direction to move to further develop my dance career.

The carpet cleaning business was rolling along okay, but I was tired of it and certainly didn't want to do it for the rest of my life! The relationship with Laurence wasn't progressing too well either. We had fallen into a lot of negative patterns with each other and I was feeling unappreciated and taken for granted. I was really at loose ends.

Mom called and said she had a three-week vacation in September and wanted to go to Sardinia. She was recuperating from a major, long-standing love affair which had just ended, and offered to pay my way if I would accompany her. She was really hurting from the breakup and told me she needed me to be with her. I felt the trip might give me some much needed perspective on my life, so off I went.

SARDINIA

Sardinia is a large island off the coast of Italy, just above Sicily. It is quite popular among Europeans as a vacation spot, but for some reason is almost unknown in America (I've seldom met anyone who has been there). There was a small area, the Costa Smeralda, that had been developed as an expensive resort for the international jet set. Other than that, the rest of the island at that time was nearly undeveloped. It was extremely beautiful, with gorgeous beaches, charming little towns, and rugged mountains. Way up in the mountains there were even a few little towns where people still wore their traditional colorful native costumes as daily wear. Sardinia had always been a crossroads of European and North African civilizations, and there are a great many interesting ruins and artifacts dating from the original native culture and continuing through Phoenician civilization, Carthaginian, Roman, Spanish, and so on. Sardinia has its own language, the closest living language to ancient Latin, though Italian is now the official and commonly spoken language.

My mother and I both fell deeply in love with Sardinia. By this time I was beginning to embrace the possibility of reincarnation, and I had such a strong feeling of connection and home in this place I wondered if I had lived there before. My mother felt the same way and we discussed the possibility that we had been there together.

Sardinia was quaint and old-fashioned and the people were warm and friendly to us. We explored the entire island, spending a few days in one place and then moving on. Most of the last week we spent in Villasimius, a resort with a hotel and a beautiful beach, and we met an English mother and daughter who were also vacationing together. The daughter, Geraldine, was just my age and we rapidly became good friends.

There was a good-looking, dashing young Italian named Carlo working at the hotel as a water-skiing instructor for the summer. When Carlo wasn't water-skiing he was riding his motorcycle, and generally fulfilling my pictures of a sexy, romantic Italian. He and his friend invited Geraldine and me out, which thrilled us to no end. Carlo spoke excellent English and, as it turned out, we had a lot to say to each other. He was intelligent, sensitive, and intense, and I soon became very infatuated with him. When I had to leave, we promised to write each other and get back together as soon as we could, one way or another.

Geraldine and I had also formed a strong bond with each other and with Italy, and before we left Sardinia we made a pact that we would go home to our respective countries, work and save our money, and reunite back in Italy the following summer, with each other and with our Italian lovers.

When I returned to California, my absence had made Laurence's heart grow fonder and he was eagerly waiting for me, wanting to make a new start on our relationship. When I told him about my affair with Carlo, he flew into a jealous rage and smashed a big photograph of me he had enlarged and framed. I felt guilty, confused, and torn apart by my feelings. Eventually I realized that I needed to make the break. It was very painful but I packed up my things and moved to Washington, D.C., to live with my mother and get a job, in order to make the money to go back to Europe.

WASHINGTON, D.C.

I got a job working as the receptionist for the South Vietnamese Embassy. This was shortly before the end of the war, when South Vietnam still had a U.S. Embassy. Because of my antiwar sentiments I had some conflicts about taking the job, wondering if I was betraying my principles. But the job sounded so interesting that I couldn't resist.

It was the only regular, nine-to-five job I have ever had in my life, and it turned out to be pleasant and interesting. The Embassy was housed in a gorgeous old mansion on Embassy Row. It was furnished with beautiful oriental art and furniture. I sat at the front desk, answering the phone, greeting people, and directing them to the proper offices. Most of the people I dealt with were Vietnamese women married to Americans, coming to renew their passports, etc. Sometimes there were bigwig American politicians coming to meet with the Vietnamese diplomats. I loved the job for the opportunity it gave me to get to know something of the Vietnamese culture and people. One of the best things was the fact that the Ambassador's personal Vietnamese chef cooked lunch for all of us every day. For only $1.50 a meal, I enjoyed the most superb food I have ever eaten (Vietnamese is still my favorite food).

It was fascinating living in Washington, D.C., a completely different environment than I was used to in California. I had never spent a winter in freezing cold before (except as an infant) and found it rather invigorating, and I enjoyed the sophistication and the political atmosphere.

During this time my mother was going through a deep depression following the breakup of her relationship. At age fifty, I think she was confronting the fact that her relationships with men had not worked out. Like my heartbreak at age fourteen, it threw her into intense hopelessness and despair.

She wanted my support and companionship but I found it very difficult to handle being around her pain. I felt helpless and smothered and tried to focus on living my own life. She, in turn, felt angry and neglected. It was a painful time for both of us.

After a few months of letter writing, Carlo dropped out of communication. Geraldine and I were very much in touch, however, and proceeded with our plans. I saved most of my paycheck for my trip back to Italy in June.

Meanwhile, I started going out with a young Vietnamese man, a college student who worked as a caretaker at the Embassy. I've always been fascinated by and attracted to men who are different from me, especially those from a different culture. Tam was beautiful physically, sweet, and quite mysterious. He spoke English with a combined Vietnamese and French accent which I found romantic. I was fascinated with the unusual ways he thought and did things. Also, he was all alone in this country and intensely homesick for his large family in Vietnam whom he was afraid he might never see again (he never did), which brought out my strong motherly instinct.

I got the bright idea that if I married him, he could get his permanent residency and have a more secure status here. Partly out of guilt because I was about to leave him, and partly out of insecurity about my upcoming travels and a need for something to hold onto, I married him.

I'll never forget our marriage in an official's office. I was a slender twenty-two-year-old in a miniskirt; Tam was twenty-eight but looked eighteen, a handsome young Asian with glasses. The official told us to repeat after him as he read the words of the marriage ceremony, but Tam couldn't really understand what he was saying and simply mumbled a close approximation. I tried my best to keep a straight face as I listened to my about-to-be husband earnestly murmuring gibberish instead of marriage vows.

I didn't tell my mother about the marriage—I figured she didn't need anything else to be upset about. A few weeks later I left for Europe. I saw Tam three times after that—a few months later when he visited me in Europe, briefly when I returned to the U.S. via Washington, and many years later when he had moved to Los Angeles. Because we put off getting a divorce, we were legally married for fourteen years! We finally did divorce a few years ago. I hope the story of my marriage was not a statement about my capacity for intimacy and commitment in a relationship at that time, but I'm afraid that perhaps it was.

ITALY

True to plan, Geraldine and I reunited in Rome. We stayed at a youth hostel and spent a week or so exploring that city before we went back to Sardinia. We had lost touch with our Italian boyfriends, but Geraldine didn't care because she hadn't really been in love with Massimo, whereas I had the feeling I would find Carlo again. Meanwhile, there were a tremendous number of other attractive men around and we were ready to enjoy everything to the maximum.

It was fun to get so much attention from the aggressively appreciative Italian men. I knew instinctively to keep a good sense of humor, enjoy it, and not take it too seriously. We were young and fancy-free, ready to have a good time.

Geraldine was a unique being—she reminded me of a character from a Victorian novel. She was very pretty with an air of naive innocence. She was typically English, with a prim exterior, but she had a wild, fun-loving streak underneath, and a very romantic view of the world. I discovered after we had been traveling together for months that she could barely see without her glasses, yet seldom wore them because she didn't want to see people and things too precisely. "I don't like to see everyone's blemishes," she said. "People look much better when you see them through a blur."

When Geraldine first arrived in Italy, she was white-skinned, pink-cheeked, and slightly plump. During her stay in Italy she grew slim, brown, and very sexy. Our personalities were opposite but complimentary—I tended to be the dynamic leader, she the willing follower. We were both out to find adventure, have fun, and shatter some old images of ourselves.

We took the overnight boat from Rome to Sardinia, and arrived back on our beloved island just at dawn. We had backpacks and enough money to last us a few months if we were careful. We hitchhiked around and stayed in cheap "pensiones" (bed and breakfast places) or youth hostels or occasionally on the beach. We would stay in a town for a few days and then hitchhike to the next town. In each town we would meet some local guys and go to the beach, go out to dinner, go out dancing.

The culture of Sardinia was actually quite conservative and old-fashioned, probably about fifty years behind modern Italian cities. In Cagliari, for example, the biggest city in Sardinia, no women (except Geraldine and me) were ever out on the streets after 9:00 P.M. Two foreign girls hitchhiking around and acting generally outrageous must have been pretty shocking to the local folks. We were blissfully unaware of this, however, and somehow felt very safe.

Sardinia was supposed to harbor gangs of bandits in the mountains. When people picked us up hitchhiking and asked us what we were doing, we used to joke that we were searching for "banditi." Despite all our outrageous behavior only two mishaps befell us. Once was when a group of fishermen took us out in their boat and kept us overnight hoping to seduce us (they didn't try very hard and nothing happened), and another time when an overzealous mother locked Geraldine into a room trying to convince her to marry her son. (She eventually let her go.)

I had studied Italian while in Washington, D.C., in preparation for the trip. Almost no one in Sardinia spoke English, so I got plenty of practice and was soon able to speak and understand rudimentary Italian. Geraldine had never studied any grammar and just picked up the necessities to make herself understood. She always spoke Italian quite ungrammatically but was so cute and charming about it that nobody cared.

Eventually we arrived back in Villasimius where we had met the previous year. I was hoping to find Carlo, but he was not working there that summer. It was a beautiful place with a gorgeous beach and we decided to stay for a while. This time we stayed in a cheap pensione rather than the expensive hotel.

LUCIANO

One evening we were having pizza at a funky outdoor cabana near the beach. Some local guys were playing music and singing and it was a fun, rowdy atmosphere. All of a sudden I looked up from my dinner into one of the most beautiful male faces I've ever seen. A young man had sat down across the table from me. He was about my age with thick wavy black hair, golden skin, high cheekbones, a strong prominent nose and brow, thick eyebrows, enormous deep brown eyes, and a beautiful mouth. His face held such classic beauty and power that I was literally mesmerized. I tried not to stare, but couldn't help myself. We nodded and exchanged a few pleasantries in Italian and proceeded with our dinner. A few minutes later he got up and left.

For days I kept thinking about him, talking to Geraldine about him, and constantly wondering who he was.

One afternoon as I was walking up the road from the beach toward town, a car pulled up beside me. It was *him*. He pushed open the car door on my side and asked me if I wanted a ride. I'll never forget the feeling as I stepped into the car. His presence was so powerful I felt as if I were melting inside. As we drove into town he asked me to go out with him that night, and I nodded weakly and said, "Si." That was the extent of the conversation I was able to muster up.

Oddly enough I don't remember much about our first date, or many of our other dates for that matter. I just remember what it was like to be with him and that I fell totally, passionately in love. His name was Luciano (pronounced Loo-cha-no) and he was born in Calabria, in southern Italy, but had grown up in Torino, in northern Italy. He was working as a waiter at the hotel in Villasimius for the summer. As the season was almost over, he would be going back to Torino in a week or so.

It is hard to describe what it was about him that affected me so intensely. He had very strong male energy which threw me completely into my female energy—an unusual, delicious, and rather disconcerting experience for me. He was wild and spontaneous, warm and romantic, and extremely funny and playful. He also had a dark, brooding, mysterious side to his nature which scared and intrigued me.

He was not handsome in a conventional way, like a magazine model. In fact, he had a stocky build and a bit of belly, which I loved. Yet his physical beauty penetrated me to my core, and evoked images (and memories?) of ancient Greeks, Romans, East Indians, and Gypsies. I remember one time waking up in the middle of the night, lighting a candle, and watching him sleep for hours, entranced by the candlelight on his beautiful face. I felt like Psyche in the myth of Cupid and Psyche. She has never seen her husband, as he comes to her only at night, and though he is kind and loving to her, she is told he is an ugly monster. One night she does the forbidden thing—she lights a candle as he lies sleeping beside her, so she can confirm her worst fears. To her amazed delight, she finds he is incredibly beautiful, and gazes at him in breathless adoration.

Luciano spoke fluent Italian and French but no English, so our verbal communication was limited to my very basic Italian. This was kind of frustrating at times, but it did add to the romantic mystery of it all, and of course we had other more important modes of communication. The language barrier could at times be hilariously funny as we attempted to find ways to make ourselves understood. Luciano loved American rock 'n roll and knew some of the words without knowing what they meant. I'll never forget him looking at me with big, innocent eyes and asking, "What does it mean, shake-it-up-baby-now?" Or overhearing him mumbling the words to John Lennon's song, "Imagine all the peefles . . ."

We had a week or so of intense passion and wonderful fun, and then Luciano had to leave. He was acting a bit mysterious, and I couldn't understand Italian well enough to grasp exactly why he had to leave, but he seemed quite troubled about his future and I gathered he needed to go back home and get a good job. We promised to stay in touch and see each other again when we could. It was hard to let him go, but I felt sure we would be together again soon.

It was October, the summer season was over, and Geraldine and I were running low on money. Geraldine decided she needed to return to England to work for the winter so she could save the money to come back the following summer. She invited me to come with her for a while.

We took the train and boat back to England. Geraldine lived with her mother just outside of Oxford, in a several-hundred-year-old house that was delightfully modernized on the inside. Everything was so quaint and charming I could hardly believe it.

Geraldine's aunt ran a home for wealthy elderly ladies located in an old stone mansion right on the grounds of Blenheim Palace, home of the Duke of Marlborough. She offered me a job assisting her in caring for the house and the old ladies, for which I received room, board, and a small salary. It was freezing cold, damp and foggy, and there was no central heating in the house. But the cook served wonderful meals of roast beef or pork, fresh cooked vegetables from the garden, and all kinds of fresh apple pies, puddings, etc. One of my tasks was to take the aunt's overly energetic young dog for long walks on the gorgeous grounds of the palace, where there were herds of sheep and cattle, little bridges over streams, and wild pheasants, all enshrouded in fog. It was so picturesque—an interesting and charming slice of English country life.

However, I was lonely, and pined for Luciano. I had written him but two months went by and I didn't hear a word from him. Finally a letter arrived saying he had found a job in Torino and wanted very much to see me. I was tired of the cold in England and decided to go back to Rome and see if I could get a job there. I took a train to Paris for a few days, where I had a marvelous time at the museum of impressionist paintings. Then on Christmas Eve I took the overnight train to Torino, where Luciano met me on Christmas morning. It was wonderful to see him, and he took me to meet his family.

His mother was a classic Italian mama—plump, pretty, warm, and angelically sweet. He obviously adored her. He had twin sisters who were both married; one sister and her husband put me up in their apartment. After months of being on the road and my lonely stay in England, it meant a lot to be welcomed into this warm family.

ROME

Luciano and I had a wonderful time together, but he was a bit preoccupied with work, and I needed to get a job too, so in a few days I left for Rome. In Rome I found an "au pair" job—living with a family and taking care of their children. They were a wealthy psychiatrist, his wife, and their four children, and they lived in a large elegant apartment. I had my own room, board, and a small salary. I saw the kids off to school in the morning, had a few hours off, then needed to be there in the afternoons and evenings to take care of them. None of the family spoke any English, so my Italian improved rapidly.

I found an American dance teacher who gave wonderful modern dance classes, and I began taking her classes in the mornings. I loved getting back into dance, and loved living in Rome. In the summer Rome had been hot and full of tourists, but in the winter it was beautiful. I loved the ancient feeling of the city—you would just turn a corner and suddenly be in front of a wall you knew had been there for two thousand years. I felt completely at home, and I must have looked it, because people began mistaking me for an Italian.

The only flaw in my contentment was that I was lonely and missed Luciano terribly. He wrote me love letters, we visited each other when we could, and I was in ecstasy when I was with him. But neither of us had much money or much free time from our jobs. Luciano always seemed somewhat preoccupied and troubled about his life and I never could get a clear picture as to why—perhaps just the normal confusion of a twenty-four-year-old who didn't want to be a waiter forever and didn't see many other options.

Whenever I visited Luciano he always seemed to have business to take care of in which I couldn't be included. I had to wait for hours while he went off and did whatever he had to do. I discovered, however, that this was normal behavior for Italian males—in fact, he was probably hanging out with his buddies at a cafe. The good part about it was that when he was with me, I had his full attention, which seemed worth whatever else I had to go through.

A strange thing happened to me, living in Italy. Since I spoke mostly Italian, I began thinking in Italian as well. However, because I knew only enough Italian to think and speak relatively simple concepts, my intellectualism was melting away. The Italian culture gave much more support for being emotional and passionate than I was used to. For example, Luciano was quite jealous of me and expected me to be jealous of him too (I was!). It was accepted, even expected, that we would express these feelings. So it was quite all right for me to have a fit of jealousy if I suspected him of looking at another woman. I found this all very freeing. I was being liberated from my identity as a liberated intellectual! I was becoming an earthy, passionate woman, and I loved it.

At one point I felt I needed to see Carlo again, as I still had him in the back of my mind. I knew where his family lived so I went to see them to find out where Carlo was living. It was in a town near Torino, so once when I was visiting Luciano I lied to him (I later confessed) and went off to visit Carlo. He was shocked to see me, and I could tell he still had strong feelings for me, but he was distant and rather uncommunicative. I left feeling clear that the relationship with Luciano was the one I wanted.

I tried to get Luciano interested in the idea of traveling and having adventures with me, but he couldn't seem to grasp that as a real possibility. I began having fantasies about marrying him and living in Italy for the rest of my life.

One night Luciano came on the train to visit me for the weekend. For some reason he was more open to me than I'd ever felt him to be before; he was wide open, in fact, and talked to me more seriously about our relationship than he ever had. For some reason, I panicked. I suddenly felt afraid of being trapped, and uncertain about my feelings. He picked up on this immediately and I felt him shut down again.

I later went over and over this in my mind, and wished I hadn't reacted that way, or that I could have had more time to work through my feelings before he reacted away from me.

I don't know if it was that incident or something else, but shortly after that he became very distant. I tried to find out what he was feeling, but he didn't make any effort to communicate, and the language barrier made it frustratingly impossible to communicate unless both people made the effort. When I went to visit him to try to find out what was going on, he behaved strangely— I stayed at a hotel and hardly saw him at all. Finally, he left a note at the hotel desk for me saying he was sorry but he couldn't see me anymore.

I went into a state of shock. I felt completely alone, abandoned and bereft. I had tried everything I could think of to work this out, and finally I had to give up. I felt like I was dying. The depth of my feelings for him and the pain of abandonment was almost more than I could bear.

I had been in Italy almost a year and was planning to stay longer, but my mother offered to pay my way if I wanted to come home for a visit. So I got on a plane and sat there numbly staring into space as I flew home. I never saw Luciano again, but I would never forget him.

WORLD TRAVELS

In Italy I had received a fascinating letter from my mother telling of a seminar she had attended called Silva Mind Control. She said she had learned techniques for imagining what you want and then making it come true. Coming from my highly rational mother, this was an extraordinary statement. I still remember how my heart leapt as I read the letter. Somewhere inside I had known since childhood that there was such a thing as magic, and what my mother described sounded like magic! She was so excited about what she was learning that she offered to pay my way to come home to California where she was now living and take the Silva Mind Control course, which I did.

The course was a week long—five weekday evenings and a full weekend. It started off very rationally and scientifically, the teacher explaining how we use only a small percentage of our mental capacities, and discussing the research being done on using more of our mind. We were taught some techniques for improving our memories, going to sleep and waking up, remembering our dreams, and simple visualization techniques. All of this was logical enough to appeal to an educated, rational person like myself, and succeeded in getting me to relax, release my fears and doubts, and open to new possibilities. Gradually they introduced more psychic techniques, and at the end of the course they had us do the following exercise:

We paired off into partners, and one person was given a card with the name and details about an actual person who had some type of physical ailment. His/her partner would go into a meditative state of mind. The first person would say the name, sex, age, and city of residence of the person on the card. The second person would "tune into" and try to describe the nature of the subject's illness. Uncannily, people frequently were able to make exact guesses or come very close. We each practiced working several "cases."

My experience with this literally blew my mind and all my previous concepts about what was possible. In the first case I worked, I fumbled around mentally for a few minutes and then came out with the right answer. After that, I felt as if my mind sank into a certain groove, or tuned into a certain channel where all the information just came to me. My partner would give me the basic facts about a person and then the words "liver cancer" or "allergies" or whatever it was would appear to me. I was correct every time. People began gathering around me, and they kept giving me more cases. Eventually I worked ten cases and got every one right!

Later they explained why they used the names of real people with real problems to teach us to trust our intuitive awareness. They used vital and important information because it is easier to pick up than if it were presented as an inconsequential game, like trying to identify the right color or shape on a card.

I was shocked and amazed by my experience. Apparently I was quite psychic, and I didn't even know if I believed in being psychic! Interestingly, I never tried to repeat my experience—I think I was afraid to. And I never tried to develop my psychic abilities per se, although that has certainly happened as a result of the other work I've done.

I was so turned on about what I was learning that I immediately went to San Francisco, where they were offering the advanced course from Jose Silva himself. The main thing I learned from the Silva courses was the technique of visualization and the concept that we influence what happens to us by what we think about, imagine, and expect. I began to practice meditation and visualization every day and immediately began to achieve good results in such areas as minor health problems, financial matters, travel plans, and little difficulties with people. I would just imagine the result I wanted consistently for a while, and usually things would work out as I had been picturing.

This was a big step for me. I went from feeling that life was seemingly a meaningless, random experience that was just "happening" to me and that I was simply trying to make the best of, to recognizing that I have conscious control and choice over what I create for myself. It was exciting and empowering. I felt a whole new world had opened up for me.

The one thing I wanted most, however—to be reunited with Luciano—didn't seem to be at all affected by my attempts to visualize it. Even while I was doing the visualization I could feel it was hopeless, it wasn't working. I soon discovered that while the visualization technique is very powerful, it can't be used to make something happen that isn't meant to happen. In fact, often the more desperately we want something, the less effective visualization is. This is because underneath the desperation is fear, which needs to be recognized and worked with before there is a clear channel to create or attract what we desire. Years later I realized that when I use visualization I'm not *making* anything happen. I'm simply *clearing away my own resistance* and allowing to happen what is for my highest good.

I felt a strong intuitive pull to go back to Italy, although I didn't know why since I no longer had a job or a relationship. I had inherited about a thousand dollars when my maternal grandmother died, so I used the money to fly back to Rome. I found a job in an office doing some translating, and started taking dance classes again. I felt fairly contented, and planned to stay in Italy indefinitely. I missed Sardinia, though, so I decided to go over for a few days.

I took the overnight boat and was surprised to meet two very tall (both six feet, four inches) handsome American guys on board. (I'd seldom encountered another American in Sardinia.) It was their first time there and I offered to show them around. One of them—Clemente—was half Italian and was working at the American Embassy in Rome, and the other was his friend, David, who was visiting him. Clemente was a motorcycle enthusiast who owned a big BMW, and David was planning to buy a motorcycle also, so the two of them could travel around the world!

They were both exceptionally attractive, intelligent, and entertaining, and it was fun to hang out with American men again; I could actually converse with them about anything, without effort. We had a good time traveling together, and by the time we reached my old stomping ground of Villasimius, David and I were having an affair. (I began to wonder what kind of spell that place had—this was the third time I had fallen in love there.)

After exploring Sardinia and heading back to Rome, David invited me to go to India with him and Clemente. At first I was reluctant. I had no conscious desire to go to India and it sounded kind of scary. On the other hand, I really liked David and had nothing else to do. So David and I bought an old VW van for four hundred dollars, fixed it up with a bed and a camp stove, and set out for India—David and I in our van and Clemente on his motorcycle. (I think David was secretly relieved not to have to ride a motorcycle. I saved him from having to prove how macho he was to his friend.)

JOURNEY TO THE EAST

The journey from Europe to India was one of the most amazing adventures of my life. I'm so glad I did it then, since it can no longer be done easily. We crossed Greece, Turkey, Iran, Afghanistan, and Pakistan to arrive in India. We set out in late September and arrived around Christmastime. The journey could be an entire book in itself, so I'll content myself with sharing a few memories.

My strongest impression was how big the sky always seemed—

driving across thousands of miles of mostly desert, you could see from horizon to horizon, 360 degrees around.

Wondrous, timeless, breathtaking scenes:

In Turkey, a gray-bearded old man riding a donkey along a desert road, with a veiled woman walking behind.

In Istanbul, going to a Turkish bath—a huge, ancient, marble palace filled with steam and fat women attendants to massage you.

In Iran, groups of nomadic people in rich red costumes with herds of camels gliding across the desert.

The astounding contrasts of Teheran—extremely modern, lavish, western-style buildings and the worst traffic problems I had ever seen; and only a few miles out of the city, villages of small round mud huts and inhabitants washing their clothes and dishes in the river.

In Afghanistan, fierce-looking tribesmen in flowing robes stalking across the desert carrying rifles.

David and I stayed in cheap lodgings (usually no more than fifty-cents or a dollar per night) when we passed through the cities, and camped in our van the rest of the time. We would rendezvous with Clemente every few days or so. In between, he took a lot of exploratory side trips. When we pulled into an appointed rendezvous town, we would invariably find Clemente and his motorcycle completely surrounded by dozens of awestricken villagers. With his height, his handsome beard, and his bright blue eyes, he looked every inch the modern version of the swash-buckling hero.

Shortly after leaving Italy, David and I camped one night on a remote hillside in Greece. When we woke up and went outside the next morning we found a tiny black-and-white dog, half-starved and covered with fleas and ticks. We fed her, cleaned her up, and tried half-heartedly to find a home for her in the next town, without any luck. But it was already too late—we were completely in love with her, and she was destined to be our traveling companion.

She was adorable—about the size and shape of a fox, black with white feet, chest, nose, and tailtip—and extremely bright and alert. We decided she was a Greek goddess who had taken the shape of a dog to be our guide on our journey to the east, and we named her Daphne. She seemed to love our gypsy lifestyle and rode happily in the van, jumping out eagerly to explore each new place we stopped. She became our baby and we doted on her.

We also came to love the old van that was both our home and our transportation. Since she had the initials VW on her face, we named her Vannie Wanderlust. She proceeded quite valiantly across thousands of miles of desert. Every once in a while she would refuse to start, or blow a tire, at which point David would fiddle around with her engine until she got going again, or he'd go in search of a tire that was approximately the right size and somehow make it work.

David was tall, lanky, and good-looking, with glasses and an attractive beard. He was from a wealthy, intellectual Boston family (his great-grandfather was a famous inventor and his grandfather a famous botanist), but had been born and raised in Panama and spoke fluent Spanish. After spending his childhood playing with exotic animals in Central America, he was sent to high school at an exclusive boys prep school in Massachusetts, then went on to Harvard. He felt himself to be half W.A.S.P. and half Latino, and he found the combination a little confusing. Interestingly, he had been a city planner like my mother, but he felt frustrated and stultified in his conventional lifestyle and had recently left his job, his wife and young son, and set out to find whatever was missing from his life.

He was a wonderful traveling companion. Not only was he intelligent, knowledgeable, and fascinated with everything, he also was one of the most creative people I've ever known. David delighted in finding imaginative solutions to every problem we encountered (there were plenty of opportunities!). Not only did he keep the van running (no small feat), but he cooked delicious meals made from whatever he could find among the local people (pickings were sometimes slim, and we had lots of eggplant), carved eating utensils by hand, and kept me constantly informed with his research on the local customs, sights, religions, etc.

David could be very playful and entertaining. We had a running joke about ourselves as the Scarfmuch family (referring to our custom of "scarfing" up as much food as we could whenever we had the chance)—Mr. and Mrs. Scarfmuch and little Daphne Scarfmuch.

Our usual routine was to drive all day, stopping at occasional points of interest. About sunset we would find a suitable camping spot and go in search of whatever kind of food might be available in the local village (sometimes there were no stores and we had to approach individual farmers or families, asking to buy what they had). Then David would cook, I'd wash up, and we'd settle down to play chess, which had become our obsession. David played quickly and intuitively while I deliberated on every move and took forever. We were both terrible losers, and whoever lost that evening would feel angry and resentful, though trying to hide it, while whoever won felt guilty.

The trip was exciting but it was also grueling, and by the time we got to Afghanistan our nerves were wearing thin. Afghanistan was the most fascinating country I'd ever seen. It was like stepping back in time two thousand years. Except for one thin highway stretching across the desert with a few exotically decorated trucks, and the rifles carried by tribesmen, there was hardly a sign of modern life (other than in Kabul, which had a few amenities). There was a wildness about it that frightened yet intrigued me.

Sanitary conditions were primitive all along the way, but hit an all-time low in Kabul where we stayed at an inn, had breakfast, and then watched them wash the dishes in the open sewer running along the edge of the street in front! We tried to be as careful as we could, and never did get seriously ill, but not surprisingly we often had upset stomachs, and diarrhea became routine.

One of the more interesting observations for me was the garb of women in the various countries. In Turkey, women wore no veils and were modernly dressed in Istanbul, but women in the outlying areas often had veils covering their nose and mouth. In Iran, all women had a large, gauzy cloth which they wrapped around themselves when they left the house; this was so even in Teheran where they were otherwise dressed in high western fashion. In Afghanistan there was scarcely a woman on the street, and the few we saw were fully veiled from head to toe with only a small square of lace to see through.

When we got to Pakistan, we had to sell our beloved Vannie Wanderlust since we couldn't take her into India. It was illegal to sell a car in Pakistan, and it was only accomplished through a great many whispered conversations between David and dark, furtive men who kept popping out from behind bushes or buildings. Eventually we sold her for what we had paid for her. We sadly bid her goodbye and left her parked in the garage of a wealthy Pakistani home. With packs once again on our backs and little Daphne in our arms, we boarded the train for India.

INDIA

We arrived in New Delhi in mid-December, exhausted and drained from our travels. Our relationship was becoming terribly strained. It was cold in northern India and we didn't have warm clothes. Without our van-home it was very difficult to take care of Daphne on trains and in hotel rooms. Clemente had gone his own way. And David was upset and feeling guilty about abandoning his wife and child in order to adventure alone in the world, but instead having created another wife (me) and child (Daphne).

It became clear that we had to find a home for Daphne, which we did—with a wealthy Indian family who seemed to love her. I felt heartbroken, but didn't know what else to do. (A couple of years later when my mother was in India, she went to visit Daphne and said she was doing fine.)

On Christmas Day we took a train to see the Taj Mahal, then splurged on airplane tickets to get to Bombay where it was warm.

I am grateful that I went overland to India. I don't know how people who fly from the U.S. to India handle the culture shock. I'd had three months to make the transition, yet India still took some getting used to. It was crowded and dirty, with grinding poverty everywhere. I got used to the smell of human excrement, because it existed everywhere in the cities (people living in the streets have no bathrooms). I saw uncountable numbers of human deformities, and David saw dead bodies in the streets a couple of times.

Yet there was also incredible beauty, which I began to see and feel more and more. To experience India, it's as if one has to partially close one's outer eyes and allow an inner eye to open. The Indian culture is spiritually based and has denied the reality of form, which is why form is in such bad shape there! On the other hand, western culture, which is based on form, has largely denied spirit, which is why we are technologically rich and spiritually impoverished. Both are out of balance and will destroy themselves if integration is not achieved. That is why East and West must now learn from each other.

For my western mind, India was an amazing teacher of spirit. I felt something inside of me gradually opening to feel and perceive the richness of another reality. A beautiful and graphic illustration of this process is contained in the film *Phantom India* by Louis Malle. In this six-hour documentary, the western director arrives in India and, initially horrified by the chaos and poverty, focuses on the political situation and possible solutions to the problems. Gradually, he begins to relax and open to other aspects of the experience. The middle section of the film has an almost trance-like quality as he takes a walking journey through southern India with only a hand-held camera, coming fully into each moment, truly taking in the beauty of everything around him. When he returns from this journey he shakes himself out of the trance, but has clearly been changed by it.

Many people have asked me what gurus I studied with in India. In fact, I visited no spiritual masters. I feel that the spirit of India herself was my guru.

I had come to India with a backpack full of clothes, but soon realized I had too much stuff. I sold my backpack and most of my clothes, and bought a small canvas shoulder bag in which I could carry a toothbrush, underwear, and a blouse (I kept only one skirt and two blouses). Other than that I had only a thick cloth rolled up as a bedroll. I loved the feeling of freedom it gave me to have almost no possessions, to be unhampered by "stuff." And I liked the feeling that I could survive with almost nothing; it made my spirit feel free, as if I could go anywhere at anytime. It felt natural and familiar, too—as if I had lived that way before. I wondered if in another life I might have been a wandering saddhu—an Indian holy person who gives up all possessions and wanders freely, trusting that he will live on what life brings him.

INTERLUDE IN GOA

After exploring Bombay for a while, we took a boat to Goa—a small state in India which, until fairly recently, belonged to Portugal. Goa is right on the ocean, with miles of beautiful tropical beaches and tiny villages set back in the jungle. For some reason, the Goan people were exceptionally friendly and open-minded, and the place had become a haven for western hippies, who lived on the beaches or in the villages and ran around nude. For five dollars a month you could rent a house, have a plentiful supply of tropical fruit and fresh fish, and indulge in all the marijuana and hashish you could smoke. The Goans were cheerfully tolerant of all this, possibly in part because it benefitted them financially.

David and I rented a house that was larger than most for ten dollars a month. It had one large room, a kitchen area, and a large front porch. There was a stove, but no other furniture. To sleep, we simply put a cloth down on the concrete floor and slept on that. It was warm and pleasant day and night. There was a gorgeous beach a few steps from our door, and a little outdoor tea shop nearby that served delicious food.

It was paradise. There was absolutely nothing to do in Goa except relax, so we began to recuperate from our arduous journey. The only times it was less than idyllic were when occasional Indian tourists from other parts of the country (always male) would make their way along the beach, fully clothed including shoes, and take photographs of the naked western girls! They were irritating but we learned to ignore them.

In Goa we met many Westerners who had been living in India for years, spending winters in Goa and summers up in the beautiful mountains of northern India. Some of them were knowledgeable about Indian culture and religions, and as they all knew how to survive well, we picked up quite a few tips.

To get to town from the village where we were living, we had to walk for several miles on a path (there was no road and no vehicle could reach the jungle village), and then ford a river that ran into the ocean. If you happened to arrive at the river at high tide, you had to swim across. If you were carrying supplies from town, you simply had to wait a few hours for the tide to go down.

This was my first experience of having to adjust myself so completely to the rhythms of nature, and I loved the feeling it gave me of being a natural, tuned-in part of the earth, rather than separate from nature as I had felt most of my life. Since then, I've had a strong desire to live once again in a place that I'd have to ford a river to get to.

In a recurrent dream I have, I'm journeying to a place accessible only by swimming through water. Therefore, I can take nothing with me. The feeling in the dream is that the place I'm going to is unbelievably magical and wonderful, and feels like home.

I loved living in Goa, but living with David was becoming more and more difficult. He was feeling tied down by the relationship and increasingly resentful toward me. We finally decided he needed to go his own way for a while. I would remain in Goa while he went down to explore Sri Lanka. We agreed to reconnect in Madras in a month's time (he would wire me where to meet him) and see where things stood at that point.

So David took off and I found a woman to share my house

with me. I was more than a little upset that I had followed this man to India, only to feel abandoned by him there. I had no idea whether we'd really get back together or not, yet I had no choice but to make the best of it. Fortunately I was in a lovely environment where it was easy to do that. I turned inward to find some sense of security within myself, and spent the rest of my time in Goa on a profound spiritual quest.

Someone loaned me *A Lazy Man's Guide to Enlightenment*. I loved the book and found so much comfort in it that when it was time to return it to its owner, I spent two days copying the whole thing in longhand so I could keep it with me!

One of the most beautiful memories of this time is of a trip I took with a few friends along the coast of Goa. We walked naked for a whole day along the beaches, arriving at nightfall at the remote northern end of Goa where we slept on the beach under the stars. I'll never forget the next day, floating lazily down a river from the jungle to the sea, the haunting sound of Indian music drifting on the breeze, then rounding a corner to see a beautiful girl sitting on a rock by the river, singing and playing the tambura. It was all very dreamlike, but it really happened.

INDIA AND ON AROUND

The time in Goa floated by, and at the arranged time I left and made the long train ride to Madras. I went to the American Express office and found the telegram from David, telling me where to meet him. As it turned out, he had missed me greatly and wanted to continue our travels together.

Unfortunately, our first night together was a most inauspicious beginning for our renewed relationship. We stayed in a cheap hotel, as usual (fifty-cents a night), and were just drifting off to sleep when I felt something crawling in the bed. I jumped up and turned on the lights to discover the room was full of bedbugs. Not only were they in the bed, they were crawling all over the walls! It was really gruesome. It was too late to find another place, so we left the light on and lay down in the middle of the floor. Needless to say, I got very little sleep. From then on every time I got in bed in a new place I was sure I felt bed bugs and was always jumping up to turn on the light and look! (I never found them again, fortunately.)

We spent time exploring the area around Madras, then headed north to Benares (Varanasi), and eventually to Calcutta. We rode third class on the trains, which is how all Indians except the wealthy travel. It's quite an experience; they simply jam in as many people as can fill every available space, including the floor, the aisle, and sometimes the luggage racks. It's always hot and dusty. Yet I loved it. By this time I was so in love with India that I felt a part of it; it seemed natural and familiar to me.

We became fascinated with the Hindu religion, and David read as many books as he could get his hands on and explained to me what he was learning. It's an ancient and complex religion, not all that easy to pick up a real understanding from casual study. We began to get more of a feeling for it by hanging around the temples and sculptures. It was the first religion that had ever touched me deeply.

Hinduism has a trinity—Brahma the creator, Vishnu the preserver, and Shiva the destroyer—as well as many lesser deities. Gods like Rama and Krishna are aspects of Vishnu. Most families in India worship primarily either Vishnu in one of his aspects, or Shiva. David and I both found ourselves inexorably drawn toward Shiva.

Shiva represents the principle of change—that everything is constantly dying in order to be reborn. They say that it is Shiva's dance that keeps the universe in motion. Shiva teaches that we must always be letting go, because to hold on to the familiar is to resist the natural flow of life. If we can move with change, we can experience bliss. In India the most devoted Shiva worshippers give up all possessions and wander freely, experiencing life as it comes to them. Shiva is also the lord of dance and music, and any performance has an altar to Shiva on the stage.

In Benares, the Hindu holy city, I had what I felt was a direct experience of Shiva. David and I went for a boat ride on the Ganges, the holy river. We drifted lazily along in a small open boat, paddling only every now and then. I drifted into a trance-like state and began to feel a very powerful presence which I identified as Shiva. There were no words and nothing more specific than that, but I felt moved by the experience, and from then on I felt myself strongly connected with the Shiva energy.

Another striking experience for me was visiting the caves at Ajanta. These are ancient caves with beautiful paintings on their inner walls dating back to about 100 A.D. The energy of these caves is very mystical and David and I were entranced by them.

Calcutta was our last stop in India. It was the most crowded, dirty, and poor city we had seen. After a few days there we flew to Katmandu, in Nepal. At this point we had been in India four months, after three months of overland travel, and we were tired and a bit emaciated. We didn't have the energy to go trekking in the mountains. Instead we bicycled around Katmandu, visited temples and other sites, and hung out at the "chai and pie" shops—a bizarre phenomenon. "Chai" is the Indian word for "tea," and there were numerous tea shops that had started baking elaborate western style pies and cakes to cater to all the hungry, homesick, stoned hippies that were passing through. These desserts all looked luscious, especially after a steady diet of almost inedible hot Indian food, but unfortunately they all tasted rather strange. At that point we didn't care much, and ate them anyway.

We were both running low on money and felt we should start heading toward Japan, where we had heard you could get jobs teaching English. We bought cheap airplane tickets and flew to Burma, Bangkok, Hong Kong, and Tokyo, spending a week or so in each place. This allowed us a gradual readjustment to the western world, as each of these places was progressively more modernized and more expensive. Even so, we were not prepared for the shock of Tokyo—so technologically developed that we felt as if we had stepped into a science fiction movie. We stayed for a couple of weeks and I got to see beautiful Kyoto again. We were homesick and didn't want to stay in Japan, but we had no money to get home. Then, coincidentally, David's father was taken ill and his family wanted him to come home, so they sent him a full-fare ticket. We cashed it in, bought two cheap tickets, and flew home.

I had spent two years living in Europe and traveling around the world, on a total of only a little over two thousand dollars. The journey had been transformational for me, teaching me to live in the moment, to hold onto nothing, and to trust myself and the universal power.

THE QUEST FOR CONSCIOUSNESS

David went to visit his family on the east coast and I went to stay with my mother, in Fresno, California, to rest, recuperate, and decide what to do next. I was very tired, and so thin you could distinctly see the outline of my ribs at the top of my chest. Fortunately, my mom had a very comfortable apartment in a complex with a pool and I spent a month or so swimming, lounging in the sun, and eating Mom's home-cooked food.

By now I was thoroughly bitten by the consciousness bug. I didn't exactly know how to define what consciousness was, but I knew it was something I wanted beyond anything else. I realized that the more conscious I was, the more everything else in my life would automatically work out, whereas without consciousness, nothing else mattered anyway. So, I reasoned, rather than pursue education, a career, or relationship, I'll just pursue consciousness and let everything else fall into place. And that, in fact, is exactly how it has worked for me. Since that time, my first commitment and highest priority has been to follow whatever I intuitively feel I need to do for my personal growth, even when I haven't known exactly why. As a result of this strong commitment, I have always been supported in every step I've taken. In fact, success has come to me as a result of trusting my gut feeling and following my heart.

THE LIVING LOVE CENTER

While I was in Fresno, a friend of my mother's loaned me the book, *Handbook to Higher Consciousness*, by Ken Keyes, Jr. I practically devoured it—it seemed to be speaking directly to me and it affected me strongly. I noticed in the back of the book that Ken had a center in Berkeley where he gave workshops, and I filed it in the back of my mind to check it out.

David came back to California and we decided to move to the San Francisco Bay area, since that seemed to be the center of the metaphysical world. We got a tiny studio apartment above a store directly across from the University of California campus, just off Telegraph Avenue in Berkeley. It was a crowded, bustling, and noisy area and we felt right at home—it reminded us of Asia! Telegraph Avenue is famous for its wild assortment of street characters, and across the street on the campus there were all sorts of people on soapboxes, sounding off on various causes. On weekends, conga drum players gathered there and drummed all night and day. It felt like we were right in the heartbeat of life and we loved it.

I got a part-time job in a handicraft store and David found work as a handyman. In our spare time we haunted Shambhala Booksellers—the metaphysical bookstore—and read everything we could get our hands on. We lived from hand to mouth financially, but we were used to that and considered it part of the adventure.

We found the Living Love Center—Ken Keyes's place—and attended a weekend workshop there. The Center was located in a huge, old fraternity house just on the other side of campus; it had about twenty bedrooms where the staff lived, and an enormous living room area where they held workshops. The workshop was very intense. Ken's philosophy centered around the idea that most of what we do in life is motivated by our addiction to having things the way we want them, which causes us great unhappiness because we're usually not able to control things enough for our satisfaction. Ken tried to teach us to "reprogram" our addictions into preferences, so that we could be happy regardless of how things were going in the world around us. In the workshop, we worked on the specific problems we were having in our lives to discover what the underlying addictions were, and then made up "reprogramming phrases" to say to ourselves in order to change our perspective on things.

For example, if my relationship wasn't going right (it wasn't), I might discover that I was addicted to having David behave in a certain way to make me feel good about myself (I was). So my reprogramming phrase might be, "I don't need David to act a certain way. I love myself as I am."

There was a lot of crying and emotional release in the workshop, and by the end of it everyone felt unbelievably close and intimate. Our hearts were wide open and we were filled with love and joy. It reminded me of the encounter group I had participated in at Reed, and it was definitely the highest experience I'd had so far.

David and I had been having serious problems. He had never resolved his frustration about becoming involved in another major relationship immediately after leaving his marriage and not experiencing the independence he was yearning for. As a result, he was often resentful and critical of me. I felt unappreciated and began to feel badly about myself, as if I wasn't enough to make him happy.

After the workshop David decided to apply for a staff position so he could move into the Center. He was accepted almost at once. At that time, if you wanted to be on staff at the Living Love Center you could apply, and if they had a suitable opening it was pretty easy to get in.

I wanted to move in, too, but no other staff position was immediately available. For a while, David spent part of his time at our apartment and part at the Center, but he grew increasingly distant from me. I felt abandoned and devastated and I tried hard to use my newfound tools to deal with the situation and learn from it. I did a lot of "reprogramming," trying to let go of David. It helped some, but I still felt a great deal of confusion and pain.

I went to another weekend workshop at the Center—the advanced level. This was not led by Ken, but by another trainer named Tolly. The most noteworthy thing about this experience was that at a certain point Tolly had us (there were about fifty of us) take off all our clothes. Then we each had to stand in the center of the room and tell everyone what we liked and didn't like about our bodies. I can't imagine now how I managed to live through this, but at the time I was willing to do almost anything if I thought it would help me grow. In fact, the experience was quite powerful. After that, we didn't feel we had much to hide from each other and the level of honesty and closeness in the group was inspiring. (They later discontinued this particular process, however.)

David and I finally ended our relationship as lovers, although we still saw each other constantly at the Center. I felt heartbroken, but part of me knew it was for the best. I managed to avoid dealing with my feelings about it for very long, however, for within a few days I fell passionately in love with Marc Allen, a musician on staff at the Living Love Center.*

Shortly after that, a staff position opened up and I moved into the Center and began living with Marc.

Life at the Center was like living in the large, warm, loving family I never had. I could hardly believe I had found such a nourishing place to be. The house itself was attractive, comfortable, and well-organized. We ate delicious vegetarian food, our basic needs were all provided, and everyone was committed to their growth, so there was complete support on that level. There was an abundance of love and caring, and emotional and spiritual sharing on a deep level.

Each staff person had a specific job to fulfill—working in the

---

*An interesting note for astrology buffs: David's birthday is June 30th. Marc's is July 1st (different year). I later had two other very significant relationships with men born June 28th and June 29th. It seems I couldn't resist Cancer men born in that time framework!

kitchen, maintaining the house, assisting with workshops, or working in the publishing branch of the business. In exchange for our work we were provided with room, board, and a small amount of spending money.

We all followed a daily schedule. Early in the morning there was a wake-up bell and we congregated in the living room for stretching exercises and meditation, with soft meditation music playing. This was a deeply spiritual experience for me and I loved it. Then we had breakfast and a four-hour "Karma Yoga" period when we all did our jobs. In the afternoon after lunch we had staff training time in which an in-house trainer led us through various processes to work on our own emotional issues, almost always culminating in "reprogramming our addictions."

For some reason Ken felt the most effective way to use reprogramming phrases was to shout them, over and over again. Naturally, the neighbors had begun to object to this practice, so a new system was devised. When the time came to shout our reprogramming phrases, each person was handed a plastic bucket with a large sponge in the bottom, which we had discovered muffled the sound in such a way that the speaker could hear it but the neighbors could not. Since we sat on the floor, we would each get on our knees and stick our faces down in this bucket to do our reprogramming. It must have been a very strange sight indeed—a roomful of people on their knees, their faces in plastic buckets, yelling things like, "I don't need anyone's approval! I am enough as I am!"

My job was in the book department, doing publicity for Ken's books. At the time I saw it as just a job which allowed me to live at the Center, but looking back I realize I learned much of what I would later need to know about running a publishing company.

Ken had been a real estate broker in Florida before getting involved in the consciousness movement, and he was a very shrewd businessman. He had bought the house for very little and was able to run his publishing company and workshop business very cheaply with our labor. However, he accumulated no personal profit, was dedicated to serving humanity, and sold his books and offered his workshops at the lowest possible prices—wanting to make them available to everyone. Ken had been stricken with polio as a young man and was confined to a wheelchair with no use of his legs and very limited use of his arms and hands, so he needed constant care and assistance with the details of daily living. This helplessness and dependency put him in an insecure position in life, and he really liked having a large family around to make sure his needs would be taken care of and he wouldn't be abandoned.

We, in turn, felt just as dependent on the security he was providing for us at the Center. We were all addicted to living there; the thought of having to go back into the "outside world" and fend for ourselves again was unbearable. In retrospect I can see I was living out some of my unconscious childhood need for a secure home and family. It was a very important healing for me.

There was a free and open atmosphere at the Center at that time. Guest teachers came to give us presentations and workshops on various spiritual and psychological disciplines. We were all experimenting with different philosophies and lifestyles. Creativity was flourishing. There were two musicians on staff, Marc Allen and Summer Raven, who were daily creating songs and music to reflect the experiences we were having. The music added a great richness to the experience for me.

This living environment attracted a lot of interesting people. I formed very deep bonds with so many of them; it felt like they were my true family. The strongest bond for me was with Marc. He was a slender young man of twenty-eight with a mane of long blond hair. He had led an interesting life; he had been an actor in radical street theatre in the sixties in Minnesota, New York, and California, and since then he had been intensely studying a number of traditional spiritual disciplines. For the past three years he had lived with a Tibetan lama and attempted to follow a very strict path. Now he was searching for a spiritual practice which allowed for more freedom and adaptability to a modern western lifestyle.

I was fascinated and a bit awed by Marc's spiritual sophistication. At first he was something of a guru to me. He was also a very attractive, sexy guy, and had a wild streak that appealed to me. He was unwilling to commit himself to monogamy, however. He told me he wanted to have an "open relationship"—live together but be open to being with other lovers if and when either of us wanted to. I agreed to this, partly because I wanted to be with him and partly out of curiosity and a desire to try something different. We both had a spiritual ideal that we should be able to love each other unconditionally and love other people as well. Unfortunately, as I was to painfully discover, the spiritual ideal was a long way from the human reality.

Marc and I had a lovely bedroom on the second floor of the Center. In the first few months we were together, our "open relationship" consisted mainly of him having occasional short flings with other women. He didn't seem to take them very seriously, and wanted to be with me in the long run, but it drove me crazy with jealousy. Since one of the ideas of Ken's philosophy was that we should be able to free ourselves from uncomfortable "negative" emotions, I kept trying to "reprogram" myself not to be jealous. I used to get up sometimes in the middle of the night when I felt upset because Marc had been with another woman, go downstairs into the kitchen, get a "reprogramming bucket," and yell into it, "I don't need Marc's love to be happy. I am enough as I am!" It didn't really help that much, but I hoped it would eventually take effect.

At one point Marc went away for a couple of months to work on a music project and I had a rather delightful affair with another guy at the Center. I was extremely pleased when Marc got very jealous about it. I couldn't sustain both relationships, though, and when Marc returned I went back to him. I was pretty hooked.

On the positive side, there were many good things about my relationship with Marc. We had a profound spiritual connection and I learned a lot from being with him. We really cared for each other, had fun together, and, most significantly, a powerful creative partnership gradually emerged.

At the time I somehow knew I was meant to be with him; we had some destiny together.

One important thing I received from Marc was my name. Marc knew about my travels in India and my passion for the god

Shiva. He began calling me Shakti, which is the feminine aspect of Shiva. Shakti is life force, power, the energy of the universe. In the traditional practice of Tantra, Shiva is the male energy and Shakti is the female energy. The name seemed to feel right, and soon everyone was calling me Shakti. I've used it ever since.

Gawain, by the way, is the name I was born with. It is the same name as Sir Gawain of the King Arthur legends. Someone once informed me that it means "battle hawk." It seems a good balance—Shakti represents my female energy and Gawain my male energy.

I began to wish I could be involved in assisting at the workshops. I wrote down a few insights and ideas I had and shared them at the staff training sessions, with good results. Deva Lewis, the in-house trainer, recognized that I had talent in this direction and encouraged me to develop my abilities. However, Ken had never had much affinity for me and he indicated no interest in me as a potential trainer.

In fact, I began to get disillusioned with some of the philosophy. I had never felt comfortable with Ken, and felt he had used his own methods to repress a great number of his feelings. He always tried to be loving, but it just didn't feel real to me. As I worked deeply with myself and other people, I began to realize it's not possible nor psychologically healthy to try to change your so-called "negative" emotions by "reprogramming" them. We staff members were gradually re-working the philosophy, emphasizing learning to love and accept ourselves and our feelings, which felt much healthier. Ken was somewhat receptive to these changes and began incorporating a few of them into his teaching.

However, that spring there was a big change. Ken suddenly decided that things were too loose at the Center and initiated a major change in structure. Instead of being considered staff, most of us became students in a prototype of a three-month program that he wanted to start giving at the Center. We had to follow very strict rules and our freedom and creativity were severely curtailed. Of course, we had the option to leave, but nobody was yet willing to take that step.

One of the strangest parts of this new setup was one two-week period where Ken came up with a certain "game" he wanted us to play. We each had a partner, selected randomly by drawing a number, and we had to stay with that person for three days. To ensure that we stayed no more than about three feet apart, we tied ourselves with a piece of twine from one person's arm to the other. So we had to sleep, eat, go to the bathroom, and everything else (we weren't supposed to have sex, though) within a yard of one another. The bathrooms at the Center were co-ed and we were already used to showering with each other and living together on very intimate terms, which helped. After the three days were over, we changed to another partner, and this continued for two weeks.

The idea was to confront ourselves with our own issues. The ideal was to be able to live harmoniously with anyone, and this way we could see what kept us from being able to do that. Unfortunately, it didn't take into account the natural human need for physical and emotional space, choice, and freedom. Like so many other things we were trying to do, it was a nice idea intellectually, but the reality was something different. Much of the time I felt trapped. Like so many other things I did then, I'm glad I had the experience. The best thing about it was that my last partner in the experiment was a very beautiful man, and our time together led to the affair I had while Marc was away.

Anyway, it was clearly time to leave the Center, and I finally faced that reality. Marc and several other musicians had a contract from Ken to record an album for him, which gave them a guaranteed income for a while, so a group of us moved out and rented a big house in Berkeley together.

WHATEVER HOUSE

For most of the next year the musicians worked on their album. They rehearsed in the soundproof basement while I played housemother, buying groceries, cooking, and keeping house for them. We lived on the money from the album contract. To cut expenses, we continued to let more people (fellow refugees from the Center) move into the house until eventually there were more than a dozen people living there. It was a big, beautiful house, though, and we were used to living in close quarters.

Marc and I lived in a large, lovely glassed-in back porch. The house was known as "Whatever House," due to Marc's habit of repeating the phrase, "Well, you know whatever happens is perfect," whenever anybody was worrying about anything.

While living at Whatever House, I led my first workshop, quite inadvertently. Tolly, the ex-trainer from the Living Love Center, asked if he could use our house to hold a weekend workshop. We agreed and he asked Marc and me to assist him. The workshop went very well, and Tolly decided to do another, four-day workshop there. Once again he asked us to assist him. The day the workshop was about to begin, Tolly was going through emotional difficulties and felt unable to lead it. He suggested that we lead it.

From his background in theatre, Marc was used to improvising in different situations, so he was willing. Though thoroughly unprepared, I was game to try it. I honestly don't remember what on earth we did, but I know that four days was very long and I had the distinct feeling I didn't know what I was doing a good part of the time. And not only was I leading the workshop, but also cooking all the meals for the guests the entire time! It was a pretty crazy situation but somehow I made it through. Amazingly enough, people really liked the workshop and received value from it. We were excited by our success, and decided to do more workshops—weekends this time. Thus my illustrious teaching career was launched.

We did a few more workshops at Whatever House and some in Los Angeles, mostly with graduates of the Living Love workshops. We used some of the Living Love methods, and Marc drew from his previous experiences, but gradually we came up with more and more of our own ideas.

I continued my avid search for truth, and drew on everything I was learning to incorporate into my teaching. I read *The Nature of Personal Reality*, by Jane Roberts, and was profoundly affected by the idea that we all create our own reality. This became a major theme of my workshops. I used the visualization techniques I had learned in Silva Mind Control. I read Catherine Ponder's books and began using affirmations.

No one had directly taught me anything about leading workshops, but I went to a lot of them and copied what I saw others doing. Gradually I discovered what worked for me and what didn't.

At first I was very scared about leading workshops. The night before each one began I would have an anxiety attack and wonder, "What on earth am I doing? What if I run out of things to say? What if I don't know what to do?" I would never have done it if it hadn't been for Marc. He was always cool, calm, and collected about it. He soothed, supported, and encouraged me. Once I got into the workshop I always did well and, in fact, I began to take over more and more of the leadership. This didn't seem to bother Marc either. He seemed pleased to see my strength emerging and never indicated any competitive feelings.

I discovered that I had a talent for teaching. I was especially good at synthesizing all the different ideas and philosophies I was learning about and coming up with simple, clear explanations that people could easily understand and use. And I found I really loved the teaching process. There was great satisfaction for me in the interaction and exchange with people, and in seeing people's lives positively affected by what I was sharing with them.

Sometimes when I was leading a workshop I would feel a powerful energy start to flow through me. At those moments I felt especially clear and would find myself saying particularly profound or meaningful things, sometimes things I had never thought of before. It was as if a wiser part of myself was activated, and was doing the talking. I loved the feeling, and definitely felt that I was doing something I was meant to do.

Marc and I decided to write up a little booklet with some of our ideas, meditations, and exercises to give to people at our workshops. Marc typed it, we xeroxed copies, and stapled it together. We called it *Reunion: Tools for Transformation*. Friends began asking if they could buy copies of it so we sold it for a dollar.

THE GOOD HOUSE

The record album was completed in the spring of 1976, and a new creative opportunity immediately presented itself. One of our friends at the Living Love Center was Collin Wilcox, an actress whose most well-known achievement was her role in the movie "To Kill a Mockingbird." When she left the Center, she moved back to her birthplace of Highlands, North Carolina—a tiny town nearly 5000 feet up in the Great Smoky Mountains. She leased a beautiful one hundred-year-old house and converted it into an elegant restaurant and, as she defined it, a house of contemporary vaudeville. Collin invited Marc and the band to come out to Highlands for the summer to play at her club, The Good House. She offered to supply a house to live in and a small salary. As Marc's girlfriend, I was included as a sort of groupie. It seemed exciting and fun so we loaded the musical equipment in a van and drove to North Carolina.

Highlands is in a rain forest area—very lush and beautiful. It had a population of only a few hundred in the winter, but many wealthy families from Georgia and Florida had homes there and came up to spend the summers where it's cool when it is sweltering down below. So the population of Highlands mushroomed to several thousand in summer, and the single street in town was jammed with Cadillacs driven by black chauffeurs.

As soon as we arrived I was hired as head waitress for The Good House. I'd never waitressed before but I caught on quickly. Everyone working at The Good House was a friend of Collin's and we were all consciousness-seekers. This created a very powerful atmosphere in the place which people felt immediately when they walked in. They didn't know what hit them, but straight, middle-aged tourists would just start to relax, open up, and have a good time.

There was nothing happening in Highlands in the evening except a once-a-week square dance, so The Good House was an immediate hit. We served delicious food, and though Highlands was in a "dry county," which meant no alcohol could be served, people could bring their own alcoholic beverages and buy our "set-ups"—a glass of soda or other mixers.

Each evening would start with the band playing jazz and soft pop music while people dined. Then some very talented friends of ours—Susan and Jessie—did a set of nostalgic tunes from the

20's, 30's, and 40's. Another friend, Bobbin Zahner, sang his original songs. After that our cook, Dave Foxworthy, would come out of the kitchen and sing a set of country tunes that would have everyone in tears. Interspersed with the music, Collin and her troupe of actors performed skits. Finally around 11:00 P.M. all the older people would leave, we'd push the tables back, all the young people in town would show up, and the band played rock 'n roll while we all boogied for an hour. After The Good House closed and we cleaned up, we'd walk the mile home to our little house in the woods and hang around talking over the evening for an hour or two before we could unwind enough to go to bed.

Working at The Good House was lots of fun. I loved being around the music and the creative energy all the time. I enjoyed waitressing, too, mainly because I liked the contact with people and the opportunity to serve them. I used to practice visualizing what size tip I wanted them to leave me, and it usually worked!

All was not roses, however. There were a lot of emotional difficulties for me. Collin was a fiery, dominant personality and I had trouble getting along with her. And soon after we arrived, I discovered that Marc was having yet another affair. This upset me terribly, but, amazingly enough, I still didn't consider leaving the relationship. Not only was I totally emotionally attached to Marc, I had a strong sense that our relationship was not complete, that we had something important to do together. So instead, I started fantasizing about finding another lover who would meet my needs for contact, closeness, and honesty. I bought three greeting cards, each of which had a picture symbolizing something I wanted in a relationship. I put them up in my room and began to meditate on them as a form of visualization. Within a few days I met Charles.

Charles was a very beautiful young man, a photographer who took wonderfully inspired pictures of nature. I found him to be sensitive, warm and loving, and emotionally available to me in a way I had been missing with Marc.

Meanwhile, Marc's affair ended when the girl left town. He

felt pretty jealous of Charles, but knew there wasn't much he could say about it. I was confused and torn. I loved both of them, had different needs met by each of them, and didn't want to give up either one. Of course, part of me enjoyed having the attention of two men, but I felt so guilty and confused that it was hard to let myself enjoy it. I just tried to juggle my time and attention between the two of them.

Summer ended and business began to slow down at The Good House. We had originally planned to close it for the winter but we had all loved doing it so much that we were reluctant to stop. We kept it going through the fall, although it was losing money. There was a buildup of tension among us as we tried to decide what to do about it.

Late one night when we were all sound asleep we got a phone call—The Good House was on fire! We raced down there to find the entire house ablaze. Before anyone could stop it, it burned to the ground. Miraculously, one of the band members who was living in the attic was not home at the time. And none of our musical equipment was seriously damaged. The fire had started from faulty wiring in the heating system. It seemed like a very clear message from the universe—we had been holding on to something way beyond the time we needed to let it go!

We had fallen so in love with Highlands that we decided to stay around for a while. The musicians worked on a tape of their original music. It snowed, and I had never lived in the snow before. We had a cute, cozy little house and I loved bundling up and going out for long walks in the sparkling white forest.

Around Christmastime we decided to move back to California. There weren't many opportunities for us in Highlands, and we needed to move ahead with our lives. Charles moved to California with us.

WHATEVER PUBLISHING

Marc and I found a cheap studio apartment in a funky old building near the corner of Alcatraz and Shattuck in Oakland. Within a short time I became the manager of the building (in exchange for free rent) and we started fixing it up. As the apartments became vacant, we rented them to our friends. We had our communal living situation again, only this time everyone had their own studio apartment. This was an ideal arrangement, since most of the arguments that arise from communal living were averted by everyone having their own kitchen, bathroom, and paying their own bills! Each person had privacy, yet we could enjoy each other's company by just walking down the hall. The only drawback was that we were in the midst of traffic and concrete, without so much as a yard or a tree. Someday I would love to re-create a similar living arrangement—with each person or couple having their own private living space, plus some communal areas for socializing, all surrounded by natural beauty.

To support myself I took a few housework jobs. Because I had free rent, this was enough to get by on. Ever since my college days I had done housework off and on as a way of supporting myself. I rather enjoyed it because I could usually make my own hours and think my own thoughts while I did it. I find that cleaning is actually a grounding meditative process for me.

I began leading workshops again, sometimes with Marc and sometimes alone. Deva Lewis, our friend from the Living Love Center, now had a beautiful big house in Berkeley where she allowed us to hold workshops. Deva recognized and appreciated my leadership abilities and gave me a lot of encouragement. I quickly discovered that it didn't work for me to try to support myself financially from workshops as it put too much pressure on me and made me feel too uptight about how many people would show up. I decided to cover myself financially in other ways, and then anything I made from the workshops was icing on the cake. That way I could do the workshops from love and inspiration and the desire to share my gifts with others.

Truly, as I would discover more and more, I led the workshops primarily for my own learning process. I found that teaching something was my primary way of learning it. I was always inspired to teach the things I most wanted to learn. As I discussed and worked with a topic that interested me, I would understand

and absorb it more deeply myself. Other people's questions and problems were mirrors of my own, and as I helped them with theirs, I was helping myself too. I was learning to trust and value myself as someone who had something important to share.

Marc had been a typesetter for Dharma Publishing when he was at the Tibetan Center, and he had a vision of writing and publishing his own books. Our booklet, *Reunion: Tools for Transformation*, was still enjoying a certain popularity among our friends and people at our workshops. So we redesigned it, and Marc bought a clunky old typesetting machine and typeset it. We borrowed a thousand dollars from my mother and had a thousand copies printed and bound. Then we took some of the books down to Shambhala Booksellers, and they agreed to sell them on consignment. It was our first book; Whatever Publishing was born.

We set up one apartment in our building as the publishing company. The kitchen was the paste-up room, a large walk-in closet served as the typesetting room, and the studio was the business office. Our friend, Jon Bernoff, who had been with us at the Living Love Center, Whatever House, and Highlands, began to help us with the business end of the publishing company. (He has since changed his name to Sky Canyon.) He and Marc began recording tapes of their original New Age music ("Breathe" and "Petals") and we formed a record company branch of our publishing company. We had a small mailing list of a few hundred friends and people who had taken our workshops, and we began sending out brochures and offering our products by mail order.

CREATIVE VISUALIZATION

Ever since reading *The Nature of Personal Reality*, I had nurtured an idea of writing a booklet of specific techniques for creating your reality the way you want it. I had been using visualization and affirmation techniques I had learned from various workshops and books, and I had a desire to synthesize them into one easy-to-use handbook.

I had actually started to write it in Highlands, then became distracted and set it aside. Now I began working on it again and decided to call it *Creative Visualization*. We wrote up a little blurb promising it would be out soon, and offered it in our brochure for $2.50. About a dozen people ordered it and sent in their money.

Unfortunately, I got bogged down in my own self-doubt. "Who am I to write a book like this?" I thought. "My life certainly isn't perfect, so how can I presume to teach anybody anything?" So I stopped writing for a while and became involved in other things.

We sent notes to everyone who had ordered the book, explaining it had been delayed and offering to refund their money. Everyone wrote back, saying to keep the money and send the book whenever it was ready!

A whole year went by and I eventually felt so guilty about all those orders that I decided I had to write the book. As usual, Marc encouraged me to stop worrying about doing it perfectly and just get it done. One of his favorite sayings, learned in his theatre days from a favorite director, was "Cut the shit and do the thing!" This became an informal motto of the publishing company.

I had an artist friend, Lorena Laforest Bass, design a book cover for *Creative Visualization*. I hung it on my wall and used it as my "treasure map"—a visualization technique for imagining something as already completed. Then I sat down to write. Despite my doubts and fears, I recognized that I had an inspiration, something I wanted to share, and I wouldn't be satisfied unless I did it. Within a few weeks I wrote *Creative Visualization*. We designed and typeset it, and had it printed and bound. It turned out to be a full-fledged book, not a booklet, and by the time it came out its retail price was $4.95. Needless to say, we sent it to those original purchasers for the price they had paid! If it hadn't been for them the book might never have been written. A local book distributor, Bookpeople, picked it up and began distributing it to bookstores all over the country. Slowly but steadily, it began to sell.

ADVENTURES WITH GURUS

I continued to vigorously pursue my consciousness journey by attending every workshop and group I felt attracted to. In the time following the Living Love Center, I had some interesting and traumatic experiences with teachers.

Shortly after leaving the Living Love Center, I began attending seminars given by a teacher I'll call Margo. She was young, beautiful, and brilliant. She had been a highly successful businesswoman before meeting a powerful and somewhat mysterious woman who had become her teacher and introduced her to the metaphysical world. Margo was a dynamic and persuasive leader, and her workshops were empowering. At first I loved them, but gradually I became disillusioned. For one thing, Margo claimed to be enlightened. I was fairly naive, but I couldn't quite swallow that. She was quite seductive, claiming that we, her students, were the elite of the consciousness world. I began to perceive a lot of egocentricity on her part and I came into increasing conflict with her. Soon I dropped out of her group.

A number of friends of mine, some of them fairly sophisticated, remained deeply involved with her for years. Some of them began believing and claiming that they had become enlightened also. Eventually most of them left her and had to go through the embarrassment of discovering they were still human! For some it was not so amusing. Some of them became physically ill, and it took them years to disengage. It was my first lesson on how seemingly bright light can lead us into frightening darkness if we give our power away too greatly to someone.

I went to a weekend workshop led by a well-known woman teacher. Though I didn't agree with everything she said, I found her workshop quite powerful and admired her combination of strength and vulnerability. In fact, I began to look up to her as a role model. So I was shocked when I went to thank her after the workshop and she told me I was the only person in the group that she felt unclear with, and that my presence made her uncomfortable. I asked her why, and after we discussed it for a while, she finally told me she thought I had a lot of unexpressed emotions and needed to be Rolfed. I was so eager to do anything that would make me a better person that I obligingly went and got ten sessions of Rolfing bodywork, which I enjoyed and benefitted from although it didn't bring up emotional stuff for me (it does for many people). I never saw her again, though, so I never found out if it improved our relationship or not.

Another woman leader was a strong role model for me for a while. The first time I went to one of her workshops and saw her standing in front of a large crowd, radiating a very strong feminine power, I was struck by a feeling that I was meant to be doing something similar. At the time I had a hard time believing that I, too, could channel that kind of power and warmth. I went to a number of her workshops and eventually traded doing some housework for private sessions with her. Though I admired her greatly, we ended up parting after an incident of minor personal conflict.

I began going to workshops led by a "channeled being." He had some powerful teachings. He urged us all to recognize that we were magnificent beings who were hiding our power from ourselves and each other because of our conditioning. He encouraged us to take the risk and begin expressing our power, and to support one another in doing so.

This entity had in fact attracted an exceptionally powerful and conscious group of people around him, and I benefitted greatly from what I learned there.

This being was channeled by a very attractive, intense young man. As time went on, the entity appeared less often, and the channel himself began taking over more of the teaching. Momentum built; more and more people came to the workshops, there was a lot of money rolling in, and he was under a great deal of emotional pressure. He began to wield his power more and more erratically. Eventually he showed signs of becoming positively egomaniacal.

I parted ways with him after one group meeting where I asked him a question and he turned angrily to me and threatened to bash my face in if I asked any more of the wrong questions. I walked out into the hall and sat down and began sobbing, wondering what I had done wrong! However, I had sense enough not to go back. The group fell apart shortly after that, and the young man disappeared.

Clearly I was looking for teachers and role models, but it

wasn't working out very smoothly. I was repeating my childhood pattern of being rejected by certain teachers. Even though for the most part I admired and looked up to them, it seemed that I inadvertently challenged them and made them uncomfortable.

Despite all this I really was learning a great deal. I was discovering that teachers can have very clear and truthful information, be very skilled at facilitating other people effectively, and yet still be struggling with confusion and unconsciousness about their own personal issues.

LOVERS AND FRIENDS

I was still going with both Marc and Charles. In fact, we had worked out a unique arrangement—each one of us now had our own apartment in the same building. I divided my time among my own apartment and each of theirs. It was certainly unconventional, and at times still pretty uncomfortable, but we had all adjusted to it. The truth is, on some level, we were all choosing this situation because it seemed to serve our needs. We all had a deep fear of commitment—of being stuck or suffocated in a relationship. Yet we all wanted love and closeness. This way, both men had time to themselves, which they both needed, while still having a woman's love. And I had companionship and attention without feeling trapped in a single relationship.

Still, I felt guilty and torn quite a bit of the time. Marc and Charles, being good "new age" men, worked out their feelings with each other to a certain level and repressed the rest. Most of the time they were quite friendly, and even began working together. Marc and Jon used Charles' photographs on their album covers, and Charles worked part-time for the publishing company.

At one time, Charles had a brief love affair with Rainbow, a beautiful Filipino girl we had known from Living Love Center days. She ended up moving into her own apartment in our building, drawing the illustrations for *Creative Visualization*, marrying Jon, and becoming one of my best friends.

I had lived with Marc for two years before I met Charles, and

I continued the relationship with both of them for three more years. I was intensely bonded with Marc by a deep spiritual connection, a strong mutual love and respect, and a powerful sense of our destiny together. In certain important ways we were very much alike. We were both committed to our inner truth and willing to take risks to live by it. We both had a spiritual vision and a strong desire to share it with others and contribute something valuable to the world. We were both intelligent, creative, innovative, and enjoyed working with other people.

On the other hand, in many ways we were direct opposites. Marc was the quintessential free spirit, the magical child, more attuned to cosmic realms than earthly ones. He was the romantic, the poet, the wandering minstrel. He seemed to live under a kind of magic spell; things just always worked out for him. I was much more grounded and earthy. Marc could sometimes be a bit careless about certain details; I was the perfectionist who made sure everything was just right. I tended to be serious and very responsible.

We were wonderful creative partners. We loved working together and our opposite natures were complimentary. We shared a mutual vision and really enjoyed being the father and mother of our publishing company, books, tapes, and all our other "babies." To this day our working partnership has been satisfying and successful.

Our relationship as lovers was much more difficult. Here our differences, while making us very attractive to each other, seemed frustratingly impossible to bridge. Marc was basically a loner who needed a lot of time to himself. He was uncomfortable with strong emotions. In contrast, I was very emotional and needed a great deal of contact and communication. I felt he kept me at an emotional distance; he felt I demanded way too much.

My relationship with Charles fulfilled my need for contact. Charles was very emotionally present with himself and with me. He was very honest and I felt we could talk about anything. He seemed to enjoy sharing and "processing" our feelings and learning about ourselves in the same way I did (or at least he participated willingly!). I felt loved and understood. Charles had an ability to "merge" energetically with a lover—to become so in tune that you are acting as one flowing energy. We fell into that space easily together and I loved being with him. I often had the feeling that Charles and I were twins in some way. I think we were both so adept at sensing another person's needs and feelings and reflecting them, it was as if we were both constantly mirroring each other. I was deeply grateful for the level of friendship and support I felt from him.

He was a very sensitive nature lover and he taught me by example how to open to nature in a way I never had before. I had always been too lost in my intellect to really relate to nature (other than animals). Charles showed me how to see and feel nature from my spirit—to sense my connection with the oneness of all life through the plants, the trees, the rocks. This awareness has gradually grown in me until it is now a primary source of connection, healing, and inspiration for me.

Rainbow was another teacher for me in this way. She was a beautiful spirit who had a profound feeling for the playful, loving spirit of plants and animals. One evening Charles was showing some of his slides—close-ups of flowers and leaves, and Rainbow and I took off our clothes and stood in front of the slide projector to see how the slides would look projected on our skin. It produced such a wonderful effect that we ended up choreographing a dance with certain of the flower slides. We called our performance "Nature Spirits" and performed it several times publicly, including at the close of several of my workshops. (I was still uninhibited enough to be willing to get up after leading a workshop all day and dance nude in nature slides in front of my "students.")

About this time I met another very important friend, lover, and teacher. Late one night I was out walking Rainbow's big dog, Alee, along busy Alcatraz Avenue. Suddenly a tiny tortoise-shell kitten came leaping out of the gutter, bravely attacking Alee. I picked her up, and since she had no collar and was in a very dangerous place, I impulsively took her home. Since she was marked like a tiger and had a temperament to match, I named her Tiger Lady. She has taught me a great deal about being honestly and authentically myself at all times. Tiger Lady is both very gutsy and very loving. She has been my close companion ever since that night she made a giant leap and propelled herself into my life.

After three years with two men, I realized something needed to shift. It seemed we were all bogged down in a situation that couldn't really go anywhere. I began to feel that even with two lovers I still wasn't getting my needs met! I sensed they were both dissatisfied as well.

As I couldn't seem to choose between them, I began to think about the possibility of being with someone else entirely. Within a short time I developed a passionate infatuation for Robert—a talented musician in our group, seven years younger than I. We had a brief, intense affair, and this served as the catalyst for me to begin to extricate myself from my triangle. My first step was to tell Marc we needed to end our relationship as lovers, though I still wanted to be friends and business partners. At first he was hurt, but then accepted it in his usual philosophical way.

Very soon afterward, he fell head-over-heels in love with a young woman who seemed to match all of his romantic pictures that I always felt I didn't match. She was young and childlike, very cute and sexy, yet she seemed much better able than I to assert herself and take care of her own needs with him. They seemed made for each other—like Romeo and Juliet.

Now it was my turn to feel hurt—only I was devastated and heartbroken. True, I had ended the relationship, but I had not let go emotionally. I still had that deep addiction to Marc. His relationship with Sharon felt like a total rejection of me, especially because she was my opposite and seemed to embody every quality I didn't have. Even then I realized she was a teacher for me in that respect. She mirrored certain qualities that were undeveloped in me but that I yearned to express—especially the childlike and feminine parts of myself. I had made the discovery that the other women my men were attracted to were always strong mirrors of some disowned aspect of myself. In fact, I often ended up becoming close friends with them once the triangle was broken, as I had with Rainbow.

Anyhow, it took me a couple of years to fully heal the emotional wound with Marc. He and Sharon lived together for over six years. He and I continued to be friends and business partners, and now, fifteen years or so after we first met, we still have a loving and mutually supportive partnership.

Charles and I remained close friends, roommates, and occasional lovers for another year or so. Our relationship remained very friendly, and when we eventually went our separate ways it felt very natural and complete. He still does some work with Marc and me from time to time.

I have a tendency to stay closely connected with my former lovers and we often remain friends. In fact, people sometimes tease me about the fact that quite a few of my good friends are ex-lovers, and sometimes it's difficult for a current lover to adjust to the fact that I have all these old boyfriends around! I suppose to some people it may seem strange, but to me it feels perfectly natural. Once I love someone deeply, I love them forever. As we grow and change, the form of our relationship may change but the core connection remains. Frequently the relationship evolves into something just as important and satisfying in a different way. This may have something to do with my strong sense of, and need for, family. When I meet certain people for the first time, on a deep level I know intuitively that he or she is part of my family. This usually proves to be true—and so I find myself surrounded by a gradually expanding soul tribe.

THE MOVE TO MARIN

We had become tired of life in the concrete jungle and longed for green pastures. At the end of 1979, we decided to move to Marin County. It was hard for me to leave the pulsating ethnic mix of Berkeley/Oakland for the homogeneous white upper middle-class environment of Marin. On the other hand, I yearned for the relative tranquility of the Marin lifestyle. It is one of the few places in the world that combines new age consciousness with a certain degree of prosperity. I had been living on the edge of poverty and working hard for quite a while. I was ready to experience more ease, beauty, and abundance in my life.

We rented a beautiful six-bedroom house in the hills of Mill Valley. It had a swimming pool and a large living room suitable for holding workshops. The rent was $1200 a month; $200 a piece seemed like a lot of money to us, but we went for it. Jon and Rainbow moved into the large master bedroom suite and Charles and I and a couple of other friends each had our own rooms.

Marc was originally going to move in with us, but he had just met Sharon. We rented an apartment in downtown Mill Valley to house the publishing company and Marc and Sharon moved in there.

We moved on December 31, 1979. Since our rooms were being painted, we slept in the living room that night. We woke up together at dawn of the new decade. It felt like the birth of a new era for us. It was no coincidence that our new house was located on Dawn Place.

DAWN PLACE

I adjusted happily to life in Mill Valley. We had beautiful woods all around our house where I took long walks almost every day. The publishing company was just a quick drive down the hill. The town of Mill Valley was charming, and everything was convenient. And it was truly a relief to be out of any intense relationship drama for a while. Life felt easier than it had in many years.

Creative Visualization had been selling in steadily increasing numbers. We put a card in each book for people to mail in if they wanted to know about workshops. Since there was more and more interest in my workshops and I now had a beautiful place in which to hold them, I began to do them regularly.

I was finally earning a small but gradually increasing living from my book royalties and workshops. I was even able to buy my first new car. I visualized exactly what I wanted—a gold-colored Honda Civic—and within a few months I was driving Goldi Light.

For several years I had been feeling strong yearnings to have a child, but it was clearly not an appropriate time for that. A year or so after we moved to Marin, Rainbow became pregnant, and I found that my close companionship with her during her pregnancy and birth fulfilled my own maternal yearning enough so that those feelings didn't come up strongly again for several more years. I wondered whether the being that was trying to come through me had given up and came through Rainbow instead!

Rainbow was beautiful, and especially so during her pregnancy and birth. She was so attuned to her body and to nature that everything seemed to flow smoothly for her. She gave birth in our home with all of us around her. It was the only birth I had witnessed and it was quite an amazing experience. She was able to surrender so deeply into the intensity of the experience that she didn't experience it as painful. She didn't scream or cry, just concentrated very intensely for about twelve hours, with Jon, the midwife, and the rest of us loving and supporting her. By the time the baby emerged we were all so high we felt like we were on drugs. I actually felt that spiritual energy was pouring through from the "other side" as this being made its transition into the physical world. A beautiful little girl named Sienna was born.

I had watched my cat, Tiger Lady, give birth not long before, and she purred all the way through the entire experience. Watching her and watching Rainbow made me feel that birth is meant to be an ecstatic experience. Through no fault of our own, most modern women have lost touch with the ability to give birth naturally and easily. I haven't yet had a child, though I definitely want to. I don't know if I am as tuned in as Rainbow or Tiger Lady, but I'm grateful for their inspiration.

SHIRLEY

While I was still living in Oakland someone told me about a

woman named Shirley Luthman who led a regular weekly consciousness group in Marin. As soon as I heard about it something vibrated in me and I knew immediately that I wanted to check it out. Her groups were held on Tuesday morning and you could attend on a drop-in basis. I went the following Tuesday.

The group was held in the large hall of a beautiful church on a Marin hillside. There were about a hundred people there. Standing in front was a slender, attractive, sophisticatedly dressed woman with curly red hair. She spoke informally for a while and then people asked questions. She was dynamic and articulate. Much of what she said went over my head, which was an unusual experience for me. I usually grasp concepts very quickly, but some of her terminology was unfamiliar to me. I left feeling I hadn't really understood it, but I was intrigued.

I went back the next week.

This time I clicked into some kind of groove and understood perfectly what Shirley was saying. It had to do with trusting yourself, trusting your intuition and being willing to act on it, taking the risk of living every minute of your life from that place of inner knowingness and connection with the power of the universe. There was something about the way Shirley said things that was totally different from anything I'd heard before. She talked about living your truth in a very practical way in every aspect of your life, and gave us specific examples of how to do that.

By the middle of the two-hour session, I felt my body humming intensely with all the energy that was moving through it. That same energy was vibrating through the whole room. I left feeling exhilarated and excited, as if I'd come "home." There was something so unique and right about what I'd heard and experienced there.

From that day on I went to her group every week; in fact, I practically lived for her group. I loved the intensity and clarity of the energy I felt there so much that I wished it would happen every day. I began to take as many of my friends as were willing to go, and we spent hours talking about Shirley's ideas and how to apply them in our lives.

Shirley had been a family therapist. She was quite well-known and respected in her field, having written several books and co-founded a family therapy institute. In recent years she had moved more and more into the metaphysical arena and had stopped doing therapy altogether. She combined a deep faith in the power of God with profound knowledge of the psychological inner work-ings of human beings. She was an extremely brilliant woman, and was definitely channeling information from a higher source. What I respected most about her was that her knowledge was gained primarily from working with people in therapy, dealing with real issues. She told us that in doing family therapy she had found you quickly get to a place where none of the rules apply, and you have to throw them out and start moving on your intui-tion. She had honed her intuition to a fine-tuned instrument.

To me, Shirley's name had the appropriate double meaning of "surely." She was more sure of herself than anyone I had ever met. Since I have a strong tendency to doubt and question myself, she set a good example for me to learn to trust my intuition and my feelings more. In fact, she emphasized self-trust and self-assertion in her groups and modeled an attitude toward life that went something like this:

Know that you have the power of the universe inside you. Learn to listen to that power by trusting your own energy and your own core feelings. Back up your intuitive feelings by acting on them moment-to-moment as much as you can. Assert and live by your truth, and then take everything that happens to you as feedback about how accurately you're following your energy. As-sume that everything that happens to you is basically affirmative support from the universe on your journey into your true power.

One of the most valuable concepts I received from Shirley was that of the male and female within. She taught us to look at our intuitive self as our inner female, and our ability to take action as our inner male. As she explained it, the function of the inner female was to receive and give us the wise guidance of the universe, while the function of our male energy was to assert that truth by putting it into action in the world. This simple metaphor helped me to understand and clarify many things in my life, including my relationships. My version of some of the ideas I got from Shirley is contained in my book, *Living in the Light*.

Shirley's teaching and her influence were empowering for me. I developed the habit of listening to my intuitive guidance, trusting it, and acting on it. I learned to assert myself more directly and express myself more clearly. And I began to acknowledge myself as a powerful person and a creative channel of universal energy.

Shirley ran her group in a spontaneous way. She usually started each week by sharing with us her latest thoughts, or her latest experiences and her interpretation of those experiences. Oftentimes she gave interesting metaphysical explanations for world events, or for a new movie. Then she usually answered people's questions or gave them personal feedback. Sometimes Shirley would role-play with someone, demonstrating how to handle certain situations in our lives. At times people in the group discussed issues they were having with each other and Shirley facilitated them. And occasionally we would sit in silence, feeling the energy and waiting for whatever was supposed to happen next to emerge. From Shirley's example I learned to lead groups spontaneously, trusting and following my own intuitive feelings and the energy of the group itself. I found that the more I could let go of planned structure and move with the group energy, the more interesting and powerful my workshops became.

There were certain people who had been coming to her group for several years and were a kind of inner circle. Other people came and went, some only a few times, others off and on for months and years. I never missed a group for any reason. After I had been going for about a year, Shirley doubled the price from ten to twenty dollars per group, and many people stopped coming at that point (though many others began coming later). That was a lot of money for me at that time, but I knew there was no question that I would continue attending. At that point it was very clear to me that my first priority was my consciousness growth—even before food and rent, if necessary. I intuitively knew that that degree of commitment to myself would bring me everything I wanted in life. Interestingly enough, that was the turning point in my financial affairs. From then on my prosperity gradually increased.

The regulars used to have lunch with Shirley after the group and eventually I began to join them. Everyone around Shirley was in awe of her and I was certainly no exception. In person she was quite friendly and cordial and enjoyed chit-chatting about various things, but her energy with the group was clearly that of a queen or superstar, and we all accorded her due respect. In fact, the luncheon scene was interestingly reminiscent of a royal banquet, with Shirley always at one end of the table surrounded by her favorites, and those shyer or less in favor seated progressively toward the farther end.

The relative formality of Shirley's social circle was hard for me to adjust to after the warmth and closeness I was used to in my communal family. I kept wanting to loosen things up a little and create more intimacy, but I could never figure out how to do it. I sometimes had private sessions with Shirley and she was always warm and supportive in those sessions, and they were extremely helpful to me. I wanted to make more personal contact with her outside of the sessions, but her extreme self-assuredness and seeming lack of vulnerability intimidated me. I felt like a child around her.

I continued to attend the group faithfully for five years. I dedicated every Tuesday to Shirley, and later, when the group was held twice a week, many Saturdays too. Although I was becoming increasingly successful with my own book and workshops, my personal life centered around Shirley's group. I spent most of my time with people from the group. Whenever a question or problem came up in my life I asked Shirley what to do about it. I even bought my clothes with the idea of wearing them to the group (we were all very clothes conscious).

I liked the feeling of belonging to a kind of exclusive metaphysical club. I felt that Shirley was on the leading edge of consciousness (which in many ways she was) and that those of us smart enough to recognize it were an elite crowd. I felt strongly bonded to everyone in the group through a common sense of purpose. We knew we had the power to transform ourselves and the world, and we were doing it. It was exhilarating.

As time went on, certain dynamics in the group increasingly began to bother me. Even though we were learning to trust our own knowingness, those of us who stayed in the group developed the habit of asking Shirley for guidance on practically every detail of our lives.

Although we were becoming extremely empowered in other areas, in relation to Shirley we all gave our power away to her totally. I sensed that some people were getting caught in an increasingly dependent role.

As usual, I tried to question things I didn't agree with. Sometimes I even tried to disagree with Shirley. Whenever I did, most of the group reacted with anger toward me. Shirley's point of view always prevailed; dissent was definitely not encouraged. I usually ended up assuming that I must be wrong. Yet a nagging feeling inside of me kept telling me something was off.

Shirley and I had an interesting and difficult relationship. I really loved her very much, and I felt that on a deep level she loved me, too. I also admired and respected her enormously—she was the most important teacher I ever had. But I could never seem to do what most of her other disciples did. They trusted her completely beyond even themselves. Something kept fighting in me to trust my own sense of things even when it differed from Shirley's, including my sense that there were areas in which she was unclear.

Shirley once said to me that I needed either to surrender totally to her, or trust myself completely, but stop sitting on the fence. I went home and threw up for about twenty-four hours after she said that—I was in agony because I couldn't do either. I knew instinctively that I had to choose trusting myself, but I wasn't ready to let go of my dependency on Shirley. I needed to feel the reassurance of having somebody ahead of me on the path, somebody who knew more than I did, who I could go to for answers. It took me a few more years before I was ready to let go of that.

Meanwhile I was in my usual position with a teacher. I was sort of her problem child—the black sheep of the inner circle. People respected me but felt a little uncomfortable with me, too. Since expressing my dissenting opinions and feelings got me in trouble, I learned to hold them in, but that made me feel increasingly critical and resentful. I'm sure Shirley felt judged and un-appreciated by me.

I still longed to bridge the gap between us and become honest friends with her, but I couldn't seem to find the key to doing that. I had (and still have) the desire to give something back to her for all that she gave to me, but again, I was not able to find a way. Since I couldn't give her my truth, it seemed I had nothing to give.

I became increasingly disillusioned with the group, and disagreed with or couldn't relate to some of Shirley's newer ideas. I began to dislike the elitism and the fact that people were judged and put down when they left the group, as if following one's own energy was inferior to following Shirley's energy. I felt people who had been in the group for a long time were beginning to get stuck in some obvious ruts.

Clearly, this mirrored where I, too, was stuck, and it was now time for me to move on. It was one of the hardest and scariest things I've ever done. One part of me felt like I might be going astray, leaving the path that could get me to enlightenment the fastest. Also, I was fearful of the judgments that would be made about me by people in the group and possibly by Shirley herself. Most frightening of all was the thought that there really was no one ahead of me on the path, that no one knew the answers better than I did, that I had only myself to look to and trust.

Yet I felt enormously relieved, too. At last I wasn't divided against myself, mistrusting my own gut feelings. Though it took me a long time to fully trust them, I began to find that my feelings and perceptions are generally extremely accurate. It felt so good to finally be able to really trust myself.

I still feel a deep appreciation for all that I received through Shirley. She was truly the metaphysical mother who birthed me into my own spiritual power.

MICHAEL

Not long after moving to Marin I began going out with Michael, whom I met when he came to one of my workshops. Michael was different than most of the men I had been with. I tended to be attracted to boyish types; Michael was definitely a man, not a boy. He was in his early forties, nine years older than I, and the divorced father of two children. He was mature and responsible. He was also attractive, warm, and had a great sense of humor. The first night we went out together he made me laugh a lot and I realized that a good sense of humor was probably the sexiest feature a man could have.

Michael was a loving, passionate man and the relationship was extremely nurturing to me. He adored me and I felt safe and loved. We were able to merge very deeply at times, and shared some truly blissful moments. Our difficulties surfaced around the area of work. He was dissatisfied and frustrated with his career and didn't know what to do about it. He looked to me for a certain inspiration and fulfillment that was lacking in his life. I, on the other hand, was excited and involved with an increasingly successful and demanding career. He often felt neglected, as if he were playing second fiddle, and this made me feel guilty and restricted. I wondered if I would ever be satisfied. It seemed that when a man was unavailable to me I wanted more, and when someone really wanted to be with me, I felt trapped.

Still, the relationship was the most stable and loving I'd ever had. Michael attended Shirley's group with me regularly, and we worked hard to deal with our issues.

After living at Dawn Place for a couple of years, I finally grew tired of communal living and longed for a more private space. A friend with a beautiful apartment in Tiburon overlooking the San Francisco Bay needed a roommate, so Tiger Lady and I moved in. Within a few months my roommate moved out, and I inherited a wonderful apartment which is still my home in the Bay Area.

Michael moved in with me for a year, but eventually we decided we needed separate living spaces, though we were still going together. When he moved out, I had my first experience of living alone and I loved the contrast from all those years of communal living. It was especially wonderful to have my own kitchen where I could cook and eat whatever I wanted without having to deal with anyone else. And the peacefulness of being right on the water was a wonderful respite from my busy life.

The apartment was expensive and represented a major financial leap. It also marked the end of my hippie lifestyle and the beginning of enjoying material abundance. Although I enjoyed it, I was still pretty unattached to material wealth. Basically, I was just following where my intuition led me. As I took each step I was supposed to take, I was automatically supplied with the amount of money I needed in order to do so. So as soon as I took on the responsibility for the apartment, my income increased enough to pay my new rent. If my income had suddenly decreased so that I couldn't pay it, I would have been willing to go live in a tent if necessary. I didn't really care where I was, but just wanted to keep having the feeling I got from trusting the universe.

Michael and I went together for about three years. Despite our efforts to resolve our emotional issues, we felt stuck a lot. At one point we both gave up on the relationship and let it go for a while. He began to have an affair with another woman—an attractive, dynamic acquaintance of mine. Of course I immediately got very jealous. He and I hashed out our feelings honestly, and he decided he wanted to go out with both of us. He was able to support his desire to do what he wanted, and stay emotionally open to me. He also was able to let me go through all my feelings of anger and jealousy without pushing me away. It turned out to be a vibrantly alive and exciting period for both of us. He acknowledged he was in love with me, but wanted to go out with her, too, and he did. The situation seemed to make him feel powerful and good about himself. I felt jealous, but I instinctively knew he loved me best, and I liked being with a man who was feeling so empowered. I felt I was being truly loved by a powerful man.

After a couple of months, the other relationship dissolved because the energy was so strong between Michael and me. Unfortunately, once the triangle collapsed, our relationship slid back into a certain level of deadness.

We eventually broke up. I went through great inner conflict about it. It was as if a part of me made the decision and left the relationship almost without my conscious choice. Meanwhile, a very tender part inside of me was heartbroken to be losing the love and closeness I had with him. In recent times we have been able to heal the wound from our break-up, and we now have a very caring friendship. Michael is now happily married to a lovely woman he met at one of my workshops.

Meanwhile, I was beginning to wonder if I was crazy. What was my problem with relationships anyway? It seemed that everything else in my life was improving by leaps and bounds, but the area of relationship seemed as confusing as ever. Little did I know that it would get even more difficult.

SUCCESS

Without any promotion, *Creative Visualization* was selling in increasing numbers, just through word of mouth. It was doing so well that it attracted the attention of Bantam Books, which bought the right to publish a small, mass-paperback edition. Whatever Publishing continued to publish the larger, quality paperback edition. With two publishers supporting the book, *Creative Visualization* became one of the all-time bestselling metaphysical books. To date (as I write this) it has sold nearly two million copies including all foreign translations and editions, and is still going strong.

Originally our publishing company was a partnership between Marc Allen and myself. Then Jon Bernoff joined us, and eventually it became a corporation, with the three of us as the major stockholders. I was no longer involved in the day-to-day running of the company; Marc and Jon handled that, consulting with me on major decisions. In addition to my book, we published several of Marc's books and, gradually, select other books as well.

Since none of us really knew a great deal about business, we made quite a few mistakes, some of them costly. These mistakes were usually made when we didn't trust our intuition, but tried to follow someone else's advice, thinking they knew more than we did. Gradually we learned to trust our own inner guidance, and as we did so, things stabilized and improved. Whatever Publishing developed a reputation as a successful publishing company producing innovative, high-quality books. Eventually Jon left the company, and Marc now runs it with the help of a very loyal and competent staff. A couple of years ago Whatever Publishing changed its name to New World Library. When I think of our humble beginnings, I feel proud to see that a successful company has been built through the process of trusting and following our own creative vision.

My workshops became more and more successful and in demand. I hired a secretary to handle mail, phone calls, and help me coordinate my schedule, and I began to hold workshops all over the country and in Canada. One of my biggest difficulties was choosing among all the opportunities offered to me, and not overworking myself—I had always had a tendency toward workaholism and now it was becoming a major problem. At the same time, I loved my work and received a great deal of validation and appreciation for it. There is a strong part of me—my visionary-healer self—that is eager to heal and transform the whole world! But I didn't know how to set limits very well. I would get very enthusiastic and schedule a great many workshops and other projects; then, when the time came to do them, I would realize half-way through that it was way too much. Still, I found I always had the strength and stamina to keep going, keep giving as much as was needed.

I did a lot of traveling, giving workshops in many cities around the country. I always traveled alone and led the workshops without any assistance other than logistical work done by the sponsor in each city. As the number of people in my workshops increased, it became clear that I needed more help and support than I was getting. Claramae Weber, a woman who had attended many of my workshops, asked if she could travel with me at her own expense and assist me. This turned out to be a god-send.

Claramae is a dynamic woman with flaming red hair who radiates warmth and enthusiasm. She gave me enormous emotional support, was so helpful to workshop participants and generally handled so many things for me, that I soon hired her as my workshop coordinator. I found that traveling with a companion was much more fun. I hadn't realized how lonely I had been on the road. Claramae worked for me for several years, and now leads her own workshops.

During this period another very important woman came into my life. I had met Kathy Altman at Shirley's group, and for a couple of years after meeting her had strong, intuitive feelings that I wanted to work with her, or wanted her to work for me. Although I didn't know her well, I felt she was the one who would be able to help me make clearer choices about my work and give me the support I needed. We talked about the possibilities now and then, but she was employed at another job and the timing just wasn't right.

Finally she decided to leave her job and I offered her one with me. It was one of the best moves of my life. Kathy turned out to be just what I needed. A well-organized and highly competent businesswoman, she is also highly intuitive and a wonderful, loving friend. She is committed to the same principles I am, and equally fascinated with the challenge of creating a successful business based on trusting our intuitive feelings, and making our creative contribution to the world.

She has been my administrator, creative partner, and right-hand woman for several years, and it has been a dynamic and satisfying relationship. I have found over and over again that when I'm open and the time is right, the universe always sends me exactly the right person to help fulfill each role in my life.

LIVING IN THE LIGHT

For several years I had been thinking of writing another book. I had a lot of ideas but never seemed to get around to sitting down and writing. I felt it would be a struggle, so I just let it go and trusted that at the right time it would happen. Finally, I began to feel the energy building to write it. For me, books and other creative projects are like pregnancies. They grow inside of you, and at the right time they come out. You can't force yourself to give birth prematurely, and when the baby is ready to be born, you can't hold it back!

A long-time student and friend, Laurel King, offered to help me get the book together. She gathered and organized my notes and transcripts of my talks, gave me encouragement, and wrote parts of the book. It was fun working with a partner and it definitely facilitated the process.

While writing *Living in the Light*, some fears and doubts surfaced. Having produced one bestseller, I felt a certain pressure to write another equally good book. The fear was that the first one was just a fluke, and I'd never produce anything else worthwhile! I began to understand the kind of pressure successful creative people must feel in continuing to produce inspired work. I practiced feeling and acknowledging my fears, and then surrendering them to the universe, asking to be divinely guided and inspired.

I was so busy that I had almost no time to set aside for writing. Most of the book was written on airplanes, traveling between workshops (I had to fight the impulse to watch the movie instead, and my sense of higher purpose didn't always win the battle). Despite all this, the time was right and the book was written in about six months. And so, in December of 1985, exactly seven years after *Creative Visualization* was published, *Living in the Light* was born.

I was very happy about it. I felt that it contained the most important messages I wanted to give to the world. There was great satisfaction in finally having the ideas I'd been living by and teaching for so many years all written down and contained in a neat little package. The book was very well-received and has sold well over half a million copies as I write this and is still going strong.

I have received countless letters and phone calls over the years from appreciative readers telling me how the books have changed their lives. Of course, it's a wonderfully satisfying feeling to know that my "children" have had a transformative effect on people's lives. The part of me that needed to make a positive impact on the world has been fulfilled.

People often tell me amusing stories of how one of my books fell off a shelf onto their head or almost literally seemed to jump out at them. The books sometimes seem like entities filled with their own life force and their own purpose, like little missionaries! I think the aliveness of their energy, and their continuing popularity, is sustained by my ongoing commitment to my own process of change and growth. Since they are energetically connected with me, they continue to flourish.

TEACHING AND HEALING

When I first began leading workshops and counseling people, I thought I was doing it because I had valuable information and experience to share with the world so that other people could benefit by it, and thus the world could be healed and transformed. Gradually over the years it became clear to me that the main reason I needed to teach was for my own process of learning and healing, and for my own self-expression and fulfillment. Quite simply, my own higher guidance was directing me to teach because it was the most challenging and powerful way for me to learn and develop. I was teaching the things I most needed and wanted to learn, and it forced me to practice what I was preaching.

For example, in my earlier workshops, when I had less experience, I designed and followed a certain structure. Once I began teaching people to trust and follow their intuition, I let go of most of my structure and began to practice following my intuition about what to do in the workshop. So I was learning and modeling my own teachings at the same time, and took risks and experimented a lot as well.

Once, for instance, I had an introductory weekend workshop with about fifty people and I provided almost no structure or leadership at all. I just mentioned at the beginning that we were going to be together and do whatever spontaneously happened. Most people were rather taken aback and didn't know how to deal with the situation. Much of the first day was awkward and uncomfortable, and quite a few people asked for a refund and left (I can't say that I blamed them). However, by the second day a powerful breakthrough happened for the whole group and those who stuck it out loved it. I never did it quite that way again, however—it was a little too nerve-wracking!

I *have* found consistently that letting go of preconceived structure at certain points allows the energy to become very alive and move in new directions, and much more powerful breakthroughs happen, for me as well as for everyone else.

Eventually, as I became more self-aware, I began to recognize that I was teaching and counseling partly to meet my own psychological needs for love, attention, and validation, not (as I had deluded myself) to meet the needs of others. This is a trap I see so many teachers and therapists fall into—the "rescue operation." We project our own psychological needs onto others and then we become the heroic saviors, secretly enjoying the position of being a bit wiser, smarter, or more advanced than all the souls we are bringing to the light. Of course, teachers are usually somewhat more developed in certain areas than their students or they wouldn't have anything to teach. But the teaching comes from a clearer, more honest place when the leader recognizes and "owns" his or her own underlying needs and motivations. I find it's okay to need and want love and approval from my students and clients as long as I am aware of that need. Still, the tendency to project my needs onto others and try to help them is a very strong one for me, in my work and in my life.

Another pitfall we have to deal with in this profession is the idea that we have to be perfect before we can teach. This prevents people from going ahead and putting themselves out there as leaders when they feel they have something to share. And many consciousness teachers feel they must present an image of perfection in order to be valid. Even more unfortunately, sometimes they themselves believe that image of perfection. Thus you get the "guru" syndrome, in which the guru believes and presents himself or herself as superhuman and all the disciples are in awe, believing the guru to be in a different category than themselves.

In my opinion, the most conscious beings are the ones who are aware of and able to share, when appropriate, the full range of their wisdom and power along with their human foibles and vulnerabilities. This creates space for others to own their own power, rather than be stuck in the "one down" position.

I learned this the hard way, through my own experience. As I became more successful and well-known, my rescue operation worked overtime to try to save and transform everyone in the world. I tended to put my own personal needs aside (usually I wasn't even aware of them) to try to fulfill the needs of others. And while I was always well-aware of my humanness, I was unconsciously pressuring myself to live up to a certain image of power and perfection. I found myself to a degree playing a similar role with others that Shirley had with me. People projected the power and wisdom they had not owned in themselves onto me, and saw me as their guru and guiding light. This is a very exciting and flattering experience, and it's difficult not to get swept away by this seductive role. I felt very powerful.

I found, though, that there was a price to pay for success. A part of me loved being a "star"—being recognized more and more often by total strangers. On the other hand, at times it could be intrusive, especially if I was not feeling at my best and wanted privacy and anonymity. I had created a "persona" which I did not always want to have to live up to. I began to have sympathy for public figures who have little privacy. And I began to realize why many people unconsciously avoid or sabotage success. If you don't know how to set boundaries and take care of yourself very well, the pressures of worldly fame and fortune can become very difficult.

For me, overwork had become a way of life, and I had almost no personal life separate from my work. However, I had no time to concern myself with this problem, I was too busy working! Many of the people who had been studying with me for a long period of time became my friends and, eventually, my teaching and office staff. So my close friendships were all closely interwoven with my professional life.

Ever since I first began leading workshops I'd always had a vision of establishing a beautiful center. Ultimately I saw a retreat center in the country with a wonderfully designed facility and activities focused around consciousness, healing, and the creative arts. Meanwhile, I needed a good place to hold my workshops and classes. I was tired of hotel rooms and I longed for a beautiful, comfortable place that would be nurturing and inspiring.

We began to search for a suitable place, and after a couple of years of searching we leased a beautiful new office building in Corte Madera, and created a lovely facility with a big workshop room, a dance studio, small group room, and offices. We named it Shakti Center. I was fortunate enough to have attracted two very dedicated staff members: Kathleen Holland, who became my office manager and kept everything in my life working smoothly, and Andre DeSautels, who managed the center facility.

In addition to holding workshops and classes at the Shakti Center, I continued to travel extensively all over the country, leading workshops and giving talks that were now attended by one hundred to two hundred people for a weekend and five hundred to a thousand people for an evening.

Early in my career, I became aware that when I led workshops or counseled someone individually, a very different energy than my usual personality came through me. I didn't think much about it because it happened so automatically. Eventually I realized that I was channeling a different aspect of my being—a powerful universal energy. That energy feels very wise; words flow spontaneously and sometimes I'm surprised and amazed to hear what I'm saying. The energy also feels extremely nurturing and loving, as if it's nurturing me while it's flowing to others.

Often when I'm working with a person privately or in a workshop, I suddenly get a picture of something I should do, or words I should say. These might seem a little strange and I frequently wonder if I should really act on what's coming to me. It could be anything from touching a certain part of the person's body or asking them if they want to lie down and put their head in someone's lap, to having them stand up and make a certain noise or repeat a certain phrase. If I follow through (which I've learned to do) they have some type of strong emotional or spiritual experience.

This universal healing energy seems to come through me whenever there is a request or a need for it, and I've found that it is very reliable. There have been many times when, an hour or even a few minutes before a public talk or workshop, I have been going through some upsetting emotional experience and have felt incapable of doing or saying anything enlightening to anyone. Yet as soon as I enter the room I begin to feel the shift of energy, and within minutes I find myself feeling centered, clear and powerful, with energy flowing through me. Usually this shift continues to last a while, but at other times immediately after the workshop is over I'm back in the middle of my own personal stuff!

I love the feeling of channeling that universal power. It's as if my personality steps aside and allows a higher, more impersonal energy to come through. It doesn't feel like another entity though. It feels like an aspect of me, and at the same time a part of the whole universe. The sense I have is that this energy has unlimited power to heal on all levels—physically, emotionally, mentally, and spiritually. It seems that the energy coming through me has the effect of catalyzing the same energy coming through everyone else in the room. I believe that this energy is available to everyone of us at all times, once we learn to tap into it and trust it.

The feeling for me as it's coming through is one of great power and great humility at the same time. Above all there is a feeling of great love. I feel honored and a bit awed that I've had the opportunity to experience this power so much in this life.

NEW YORK

I had always loved traveling, and my workshop tours, while at times stressful and tiring, could also be exciting and fun. It was interesting doing workshops in the various cities and feeling how the character of each place was reflected in the workshop. I realized that different places have very different energetic vibrations, and we are drawn to the places that have the particular energy we need at any given time, just as we are attracted to people with certain energies.

One place I fell in love with was New York. I had never been anywhere that felt so pulsatingly alive. Whenever I went there, I felt as if I was picked up and swept along on a wave of creative energy. My whole life I'd had the feeling that I was a little too intense and that I needed to tone myself down a bit. New York was the only place where I didn't feel that way at all. It seemed that the intensity of my surroundings matched the intensity inside me, and I felt right at home.

The workshops in New York were often filled with interesting creative people whom I found exciting and stimulating. I felt especially drawn to the people involved in theater. One evening after a talk I'd given, a woman my own age approached me and told me how much she appreciated my work. I was immediately attracted to her. As we talked, I had the strong sensation that I was looking at myself in a mirror. She later told me she felt the same thing. Her name was Leslie Ayvazian and she was an actress, writer, and director—a very talented one, I soon discovered.

It was love at first sight, and Leslie has been one of my best friends ever since. Leslie is one of those rare people who has a capacity for deep and immediate intimacy; she is warm, insightful, funny, and has a wonderful passion for life. Among other things, I recognized in her a mirror of the part of me that is a creative performer. I realized that when I left behind my dance career, I buried that part of myself and now it was yearning to come out once more. Leslie and I began to fantasize about someday combining our talents and creating some type of transformational theater experience.

Another fascinating woman I met in New York was Gabrielle Roth, who teaches ritual theater and movement as a path to healing and self-awareness. She also has become a good friend and New World Library has published her wonderful book, *Maps to Ecstasy: Teachings of an Urban Shaman*.

HEALING MYSELF

I had achieved creative and professional success through practicing what I was preaching—trusting and following my intuitive inner guidance. I had written two successful books and touched thousands of people's lives. I knew that my higher purpose on earth was being fulfilled, and I felt great satisfaction in that.

Yet I was receiving increasingly strong intuitive messages that my life was out of balance, that many of my own personal needs were not being met and certain parts of me were not being expressed. I was so caught up in my whirlwind of activity and success that I hardly had time to think about this, much less find out what to do about it.

Fortunately, life always takes us in the direction we need to go for healing and balance. At this time I had a series of experiences that gradually opened me to my "shadow"—the aspects of myself I had buried or ignored for too long.

A psychic friend of mine gave me a reading in which she told me that all my chakras (energy centers in the body) were clear and open except my heart chakra, which appeared to her as painfully imploded. She said I knew very well how to give love but not how to receive it. I began to cry when she told me that, and I felt very shaken up afterwards.

I began taking singing lessons from a friend of mine, Pilar—

a wonderful singer. I always had a desire to sing, but felt completely blocked in that area. It was one thing I had absolutely no confidence that I could do. Pilar approached singing in an intuitive, emotional way, encouraging me to feel the part of me that wanted to sing, and the part of me that was afraid to. I would start to sing and then begin to cry. I realized singing came from a deep, vulnerable place inside, but I had a lot of armor around that place that needed to dissolve. For the first few weeks I spent most of my lessons crying, without really knowing why. Eventually I was able to sing without weeping. I discovered there is a passionate part of myself that yearns to express through singing, but also a tremendous amount of fear and resistance. I continued to use singing as a way of getting in touch with these deep feelings.

DISCOVERING MY INNER CHILD

I began to do some personal healing work with a man named Stephen. Stephen was in his mid-forties, slender, with shaggy greying hair and beard and a lovely British accent. He was from Scotland originally, taught theatre for many years in Canada, and had been on a long journey of spiritual and emotional healing. He had great depth, was very perceptive, and carried the energy of the quintessential wise man.

In my first session with him, as I was discussing something I suddenly found myself crying uncontrollably. It was surprising and kind of embarrassing as I had thought I was feeling pretty good. In subsequent sessions, I began to realize there was a part of me that was deeply unhappy. My life was so busy and successful I didn't have time to notice my pain. My entire life had conditioned me to be strong, competent, and in control, and my years with Shirley had given me so much reinforcement for my power that I had become completely identified with that aspect of my being. The fact that I was now a well-known consciousness teacher helped to lock that identity into place.

I saw myself as powerful, confident, and consciously developed—all of which was true. But there was another side of me that had become deeply buried. This was the feeling, vulnerable part, the part that let me know I had emotional needs that were not being met, and wounds from the past that needed healing.

The big trouble spot in my life was in my relationships with men. Everything else in my life was working well, yet I was still suffering heartache, pain, and confusion in my relationships. Of course I knew that I had unresolved pain from my childhood— the issue of the early separation from my father, and having to become a responsible adult at a young age—but now I began to actually feel the hurt and pain I was holding inside.

Stephen had a lot of fatherly energy. He was very accepting and created an extremely safe space for me to become aware of my feelings. I began to experience a very frightened and sad child inside of me who was so young that she had no words. I realized I had emotionally abandoned her by not being aware of her needs and feelings.

I began to recognize what was not working in my life. I was so caught up in my career and in giving to the world that I wasn't giving much to myself. And I was so busy being strong and powerful that I had very little space in my life for the expression of my more vulnerable feelings, especially my need for love and nurturing. It seemed that the only place those feelings came out was in a relationship with a man who loved me, and then so much suppressed need came forth that it put a heavy burden on the relationship. I needed to find other ways to nurture and care for myself emotionally.

I was finally able to see clearly what had been missing for me in the work with Shirley. It had been great for developing my power, my sense of myself as a creative, god-like being. But my more human, feeling self had been suppressed. It was always fighting to come out, wanting more emotional contact and expression, but I hadn't been able to give it much support.

I realized that only through the vulnerable, feeling part of myself could I make real emotional contact with people and experience the love, closeness, and intimacy that I so needed.

I saw how part of my attraction to groups was the unconscious need of my child self to create the large, warm, loving family I never had. In my own workshops I experienced much love and emotional contact, but workshops and classes come to an end after a weekend or a few weeks, and my inner child would feel abandoned. So I had created a more permanent "family" with the long-term students and staff I had gathered around me.

The love and intimacy in this group satisfied some of my need for ongoing, permanent closeness. But there was a problem because of complicated and entangled roles in the group. Most of the people around me had started out as students, developed into friends, and were now my employees, so there was a certain degree of confusion about our relationships to each other. The biggest difficulty for me was that rather than being part of a happy family in which I could be one of the children, as my inner child secretly desired, I was stuck in the mother-father role, taking responsibility for everyone and everything.

Now that I was more aware of my needs, I gradually began to look for ways to satisfy them within the structure I had already created. I began to create more long-term programs and retreats so that I could enjoy the warmth and intimacy of the group for a longer period of time. And I began to bring in other leaders who could carry some of the responsibility, so I could sit back and receive while they led the group.

I began to have Stephen as a guest leader in some of my programs. This worked well, since I trusted him and liked the way he led groups. Also, he became the symbolic "father" of the family. I was still primarily the "mother," but Stephen carried some of the emotional responsibility which helped me to relax more and allow my vulnerable child self to come forth.

Another person who helped me with this process was my friend Tanha. I had met Tanha a couple of years before when she came to one of my workshops. The instant I met her I knew she was my soul sister. She and her boyfriend Jon began coming regularly to my workshops and groups and eventually both of them joined my teaching staff. My relationship with Tanha has deepened into one of the most powerful connections of my life.

Tanha is about my age, tall and very beautiful, with olive skin and thick, prematurely silver hair. She is a spontaneous, passionate person, probably the most "real" person I've ever known; she always expresses and acts exactly as she is really feeling. Her intensity of feelings and her commitment to truth match my own, and I love being with her.

Tanha loved what I was teaching about trusting yourself and following your own energy because it gave her the philosophical and emotional support she needed to fully be herself. I felt Tanha deeply understood the principles that I was living and teaching and reflected them back to me in a way that inspired and supported me.

Since Tanha is very connected to the feelings of her own inner child self, she was also very sensitive to my vulnerable feelings. She encouraged me to be more in touch with my own personal needs and to nurture myself. Tanha has lived a relatively quiet life in a rural environment with a loving communal family, and I found myself envying her and wishing I could live her life for a while. Meanwhile, she was wanting to express herself more successfully in the world as I was.

Tanha and I both had unresolved issues with powerful mothers, and it became clear that on one level we were healing our "mother stuff" with each other: she was the emotionally nurturing mother I needed, and I was the supportive, encouraging mother she needed.

I became more aware than ever before how we continually seek healing for our unresolved childhood needs through our relationships. I saw how in groups and workshops, the group becomes our projected family, and we begin acting out the roles we did in our original family. If we do this unconsciously, we simply get ourselves into the same stuck patterns over and over until we become aware of them. Once we have some insight, we can use the relationship or the group to help us heal and resolve old patterns.*

---

*One of the best books I have read on the subject of healing ourselves through relationships is *Getting the Love You Want* by Harville Hendrix. Although it's geared toward married couples, it contains valuable insights for everyone.

On some level, one of the roles I had taken in my original family was that of emotional caretaker to my parents. I tried to heal their pain and be grown-up enough not to depend on them to help me deal with my own. So I created a life-long pattern as healer and caretaker of other people. Now I was finally beginning to get in touch with the feelings I had buried and was letting them out.

My workshops always change as I change, and reflect whatever I'm currently working on. At that point in my life my groups became emotionally intense. We created a safe space for people to delve into emotions they had never allowed themselves to feel—to accept, express, and release them. At certain times there would be an entire roomful of a hundred or more people, all crying, screaming, laughing, or whatever. It was cathartic and powerfully healing. At other times the energy would be soft and nurturing, as people expressed long-hidden feelings of fear or sadness and received the acceptance and love from the group that they had not received as a child.

I saw that one of our primary needs as children is to be able to experience and express our feelings and have someone else simply understand how we are feeling without trying to suppress or change it. A child needs to be allowed to express his or her honest feelings and have someone say (in words, or just vibrationally), "Yes, I understand how you feel." And of course, it is important for a child to have a parent who can model emotional authenticity by expressing honestly how he or she feels. Many parents try so hard to be "perfect" that they don't let their children see them as real human beings, or they have so much trouble with their own unmet emotional needs that they are not able to be there emotionally for their children. Many children, like myself, begin taking care of their parents' unconscious emotional needs at an extremely early age, often in infancy.

Even the most conscientious of parents are unable to meet all of their children's emotional needs, take care of their own needs, and handle all their worldly responsibilities at the same time. Caring for a child is very demanding, and parents are only human.

One way or another, children in our culture get the message:

"Don't feel what you are feeling. Don't have too many needs because there is nobody available to help you meet them." We bury our feelings and try to live up to the image we've been presented as the appropriate way to be. The message throughout our culture is, "Don't feel too much, too deeply, too intensely. Feelings are dangerous. They lead you out of control."

However, feelings don't go away because we want them to or because someone doesn't approve of them. In fact, feelings are completely uninfluenced by our will, and aren't right or wrong, good or bad. Feelings simply are. They are an important part of us. You can suppress them, but you can't change them or dissolve them. And if you suppress them, eventually they create problems. They burst out at inappropriate moments with many times the intensity of the original emotion, or they push you into addictive behavior, or they make your body ill (or all of the above).

Paradoxically, if you simply accept and experience your feelings—all your feelings, fully—they change of their own accord. Accepting a feeling gives it space and allows it to move. If you let yourself feel sadness fully and move all the way into and through it, you come to a peaceful feeling, followed by a lightness. Your heart is open and you feel more love. If you let yourself feel anger fully in your body and accept and enjoy the feeling (finding an appropriate way to express it, if necessary), you feel more empowered and eventually the anger passes and you feel strong and centered. If you allow yourself to feel your fear, and ask for comfort and love from a trusted person or from the universe, you eventually feel safer and stronger.

I often tell people in workshops that feelings are like the weather—constantly changing, and quite beautiful in their variety. If it were always sunny and exactly the same temperature, we would miss so many of the different and equally important moods of existence. And if we resisted the weather every time it changed, we'd lead a life of resisting the inevitable, which is what most of us tend to do with our feelings.

On the other hand, if we enjoy walking in the rain, or curling up in bed when it's stormy outside, or going out and playing in the snow, we can live the full spectrum of life's experiences. When we fully allow ourselves to feel all of our feelings, we experience the full passion of life.

Mother

During all the years I had been on a spiritual path, my mother had been evolving along her own parallel path. After introducing me to Silva Mind Control, she had taken the training to become a Silva Mind Control instructor. Through the visualization techniques, she had healed herself of arthritis, and had dissolved some gallstones that a doctor had told her needed to be removed surgically. (When the doctor saw the "before" X-rays with gallstones and the "after" X-rays without gallstones, he refused to believe it and said the X-rays must have been mixed up!)

She continued to practice yoga regularly, too. The year after I came back from India, she retired from her city planning career at the age of fifty-five and made her own pilgrimage to India, where she studied Vipasana meditation and received certification as a yoga instructor.

From that time on she became a gypsy and traveled almost constantly. She stayed with people in exchange for teaching them yoga, and led meditation and yoga retreats in various places. She made friends all over the world.

At one point she went to visit a remote beach in Australia where there was a group of wild dolphins who, for whatever reason of their own, had been coming in to the beach and actually allowing people to touch and feed them. It was the only place in the world where such a thing had happened regularly for many years.

Mom fell in love with the dolphins, and got to know each of them by name and personality. After that she returned every year to visit them, see their new babies, and so forth. They became her family. She described making contact with the dolphins as being very blissful and wrote a book about her experiences with them— *The Dolphins' Gift.*

For many years Mom had no home. She left all her possessions in storage and came back for a few months every year to visit me and her friends in California, then was off again, camping across the United States or island hopping in the Pacific or visiting her beloved dolphins. She managed to do this on a very limited retirement income by camping or staying with her many friends.

When my mother came to visit me, she often participated in my workshops and other programs, both as a student and on my staff. I was pleased to have her so interested and involved in my work, and of course many people were amazed and inspired by the fact that I had a mother who would actually come to my workshops. There were problems, however. We seemed to be encountering an increasing amount of pain and difficulty in our relationship. Mom often felt hurt and angry with me, feeling that I wasn't appreciating her or including her in my life enough. I felt guilty and pressured and, in turn, resentful.

Our difficulties were complicated by the fact that this was at the same time that my staff and I were all delving emotionally into our core childhood pain and using the group as a substitute family. And there was no objective facilitator present: I was supposed to be the leader, but I was entangled with my staff emotionally, and immersed in my own confusion and pain. Having my mother there intensified things for both of us.

DEAN

The next man to come into my life was Dean. I met him in one of my workshops. (Where else? That was the only way I met men anymore.) I was immediately attracted to his piercing blue eyes and his blond, rugged good looks. He radiated a strong sexual magnetism that pulled me right to him. He was six years younger than I, a building contractor who'd been a lone wolf most of his life. He was extremely psychic and had begun to investigate spiritual and psychic development.

Dean was a very different kind of man for me in certain ways. I had always been attracted to men with strong female energy.

Dean had that, but he was also macho. He had been an extremely sensitive, vulnerable boy who grew up in a redneck environment, so he developed a tough masculine energy to protect himself. He had worked on the pipeline in Alaska for years, ridden motorcycles, fought in bars, and generally been somewhat of a desperado. Yet I found him to be extremely sweet and loving. He hadn't spent much time with women, and he was as fascinated by me as I was with him. We were definitely opposites attracting!

Dean was the only man I'd met who seemed to really embrace his animal self—he was very physical and primal. He was smart, but nonintellectual; all his responses came straight from his gut. He was extremely blunt and honest, and had a tendency to blurt out things that other people were feeling but would never say (which both embarrassed and delighted me).

At first I had a hard time accepting my attraction to Dean. He was so different from my image of the man I should be with. After a while I realized that's exactly why I liked him so much. He was the perfect balance to my overly intellectual, civilized, nice polite self, and a mirror of the more physical, primal aspects of myself that I had repressed.

I quickly discovered he was a powerful being and quite a visionary in his own way. He grasped my ideals and found inspiration in them. I gave him the meaning and purpose he had been searching for all his life, and he brought to me an earthy groundedness and raw vitality, as well as a tender love. He became my protector. Our relationship was very much the archetype of the queen and her loyal knight.

We went together for a couple of years. Because we were both workaholics, we were able to give each other a lot of space. In fact, we didn't spend much time together except from about 10:00 P.M. to 6:00 A.M. When we did spend more time together there were difficulties. Dean had had a very rough childhood and carried some deep emotional wounds. I found myself falling into my usual mother role—trying to heal his pain. At the same time my inner child became very dependent on him. He was the strong, protective, devoted father I had never had. We became intensely bonded to each other through our mutual dependency.

Dean was addicted to marijuana. At the time I didn't think that was much of a problem. I was a child of the 60's—most people I knew had smoked pot and it was no big deal. It wasn't until much later that I realized Dean and I were hooked into a seriously addictive relationship. All I knew at the time was that it started to feel crazier and crazier.

I began to feel trapped in the relationship, and Dean became increasingly possessive of me. I felt really smothered, and began going out with other men. Dean went into jealous rages. Finally we broke off our relationship. The breakup lasted several months and was very melodramatic. At one point I threw him out of one of my groups. Another time he physically threatened a man I was dating.

We were so dependent on each other that it took us a long time to make the separation as lovers, but eventually we did. Our relationship evolved into a close friendship. Dean eventually stopped smoking pot, which made a totally positive change in his life. Over the years we have worked out an enormous amount of deep emotional healing with each other. Dean is now my beloved brother, and one of the most important people in my life.

BREAKING THROUGH MY ROLE

During this period I was leading an eight-month intensive training program called The Creative Leadership Program. The original idea was to take people through an intensive emotional healing process, and then facilitate them in developing their skills and talents to allow them to find new creative directions in their lives. However, my staff and I were all so deeply in the throes of our own emotional healing process that we never really got to the second objective. We did do some very deep and powerful healing work, but in a way we were like a bunch of children wandering around in a maze of our feelings. Even Stephen, who was assisting as a leader and who always held the father role that made it safe for the rest of us, was moving more into his own feelings.

I felt really vulnerable. It was a great relief to be able to experience and express this part of myself, but some of the participants in the program got angry at me because I was not being the good, competent mother and inspiring leader I had led them to believe I was. They felt betrayed and abandoned by me.

As if that weren't enough, several members of my teaching staff were angry at me, too. I had played the mother so strongly, and they had projected so much of their parental stuff onto me, that now I was catching all their rage. The truth was that we were beginning to separate from our co-dependence, which was healthy. But the individuation process, like the process of adolescents separating from their parents, usually involves making the other person wrong in order to find your own self.

This was extremely painful to me. Tanha, who had been my emotional mainstay, barely spoke to me for months. Stephen withdrew from me, needing to find his own space. Another friend and former staff member whom I had been very close to for years called me out of the clear blue sky to say she wanted to have nothing more to do with me, and didn't want to speak to me or hear my name again! Several other people pulled away as well.

I knew each of these people was dealing with their own process, and I recognized that this was the karma of setting myself up as a powerful leader. The more that people give their power to you, the angrier they get when the time comes to take their power back.

Knowing this didn't help much. I felt very alone.

FACING MY SHADOW

My relationship problems seemed more and more out of control. After I broke up with Dean I had several relationships which were emotionally devastating to me. All of these relationships had certain factors in common.

They were all with men who came to my workshops and initially pursued me, only to become overwhelmed and retreat once I opened up to them or fell in love with them. This, of course, left me feeling painfully rejected and abandoned.

All of these men were considerably younger than I, and all of them were exceptionally attractive, warm, bright and talented. I experienced a magical and passionate connection with each of them.

All of them were from alcoholic families and were struggling with their own problems of addiction to alcohol and/or drugs. I, of course, fell into my habitual role as mother/healer/caretaker—trying to heal them and help them solve their problems, while they were largely unavailable to meet my needs.

Obviously it didn't work very well for me to go out with men from my workshops. I had a feeling they saw me as a powerful goddess they wanted to possess, not to mention a mother figure who could fix their lives. When they were then confronted with a real live woman with intense needs of her own, they weren't prepared for it. At the time I was unfamiliar with the concept of transference, wherein a student projects his disowned power and wisdom onto a leader and then falls in love with his reflection. I was falling into countertransference, where the teacher projects her disowned vulnerability onto the student and falls in love with that reflection.

Even more seriously, I was consistently attracted to men with substance addictions, and was hooking in with them in a co-dependent role. This proved to be very unhealthy for me and also for them.

These relationships were extremely painful to me, and I seemed to be caught in a repeating cycle with them. On one hand, I would have moments of such deep connection and bliss that I would do anything to hold onto that experience or get back to it. On the other hand, most of the time my needs were not being met and I was expending huge amounts of energy unsuccessfully trying to make things work. And I was recreating my childhood pattern of repeated abandonment as well.

I had to face the fact that there was a very addictive quality to my relationships. I realized that except for a few brief periods, I had always been in a relationship since I was fifteen years old. I had a painful feeling of emptiness inside of me that I tried to avoid by looking for a man to love me.

Since I could no longer make my relationships work at all, I finally had to face and move into the core of pain inside of me. It was the hardest thing I've ever had to do. I wanted to avoid that feeling at all costs, and I would have if there had been any other way. But life had set it up so that there was no choice for me.

I experienced the depth of pain of my frightened, helpless, needy inner child. Not only had I experienced abandonment by my father and other father figures (my mother's lovers), but the overall scarcity of males in my early life had left me craving male energy, love, and attention. I felt deep shame and a sense of worthlessness, as my inner child interpreted the withdrawal of love and attention as due to some inadequacy on my part.* And the fact that I'd grown up and become responsible so young had left my child self with much unfulfilled need for nurturing and play.

I realized that my child self and my feminine side had been deeply wounded by the feeling of rejection and abandonment, and had therefore been repressed and buried. My male side had been developed very strongly—I had, in a sense, "become my own man" to provide male energy to myself. I felt very empowered in my male energy, my ability to go after what I wanted and make it happen. But I felt totally disempowered on my female side, my ability to attract to me and receive what I needed and wanted. So I always resorted to my male side to get things accomplished, while my female side remained empty and unfulfilled.

At this time I received a psychic reading from another friend who channels what I feel to be exceptionally high-level guidance. She told me that I had been replaying and re-experiencing in my relationships what I had felt as a child when the bond with my father was broken. At that time, she said, I had experienced total hopelessness about my needs ever being met, and a desire to die. I had not only repressed this helpless feeling, but also compensated for it by creating a personality that was strong enough to do *anything*. The underlying theme of my personality was "Somehow, someday, I *will* get what I need." Interestingly enough, I had

---

*I have since read an excellent book on this subject called *Healing the Shame that Binds You* by John Bradshaw.

managed to create absolutely everything I wanted in life except the one thing I wanted most—a good relationship with a man. She also assured me that by experiencing and healing this issue, I would eventually have everything I wanted.

This reading hit me very hard, but I felt it was true; I had finally reached the place of despair I had avoided feeling my entire life. It was as if all my relationships had been drawing me closer and closer to experiencing that darkest of inner places. I knew it was time for me to learn to love and care for that wounded child within me.

This was the most difficult time of my life. I was living alone, some of my best friends were estranged, my relationships with men were a mess, and I was facing my deepest despair. To the degree I had identified with the light, the powerful, the spiritual, I now had to venture into my own darkness and fear.

It was truly the dark night of my soul.

INTEGRATION

I had always been better at giving help and support than at receiving it. Now I knew how much I needed it, and I began to reach out as much as I could. There were two major influences that helped and healed me the most over the next few years—the twelve-step programs and the Voice Dialogue process.

TWELVE-STEP PROGRAMS

I had several close friends who had been active in Alcoholics Anonymous and other twelve-step programs for years. I had always liked what I heard about them, and felt that the twelve steps fit in with what I was teaching. In the throes of trying to deal with my painful relationship patterns, I began to investigate the programs more closely. I read books about alcoholism and addiction, went to meetings, and began seeing a counselor who worked specifically on these issues.

Although I had no alcoholism in my original family, I realized that I perfectly fit the description of the co-dependent—the person who is addicted to relationships with addicts. Co-dependents focus on helping other people with their problems so that they won't have to face and deal with their own.

In a certain way, in this culture we are all basically co-dependent. Interdependency is natural; it's the human need for love and contact with one another. However, with co-dependency, instead of learning to meet our needs directly, we unconsciously try to take care of someone else's needs for them, with the hidden expectation that they will take care of our needs for us. If I help you with your problems and give you lots of nurturing and understanding, then you will love and appreciate me and never abandon me. The problem is not with this exchange of caretaking, but that it is going on unconsciously, with hidden agendas and motivations.

Co-dependence leads to a feeling of entrapment in relationships. We have made unconscious but very powerful agreements to take care of and please other people, which implies we are not free to please and take care of ourselves and our own needs. Thus we feel trapped and resentful, and we are afraid to leave the relationship because we feel dependent on the other person to meet our needs.

Co-dependence starts in childhood, when we begin taking care of our parents' unconscious unmet emotional needs. The pattern continues throughout our lives unless we become aware of it and begin to change it.

I believe unmet childhood needs and co-dependency are the roots of addiction. Some people become addicted to drugs or food to fill the inner emotional void and escape from the isolation or feelings of entrapment they experience in relationship to other people. Some people become addicted to helping others in order to try to get the love and contact they need, and yet still feel in control.

I realized I was a co-dependent helper and also a workaholic. The two fit right together, since my work involved helping other people. In my spare time, I could try to fix my lovers and friends, hopefully having no time left over to face my own loneliness and pain.

As usual, seeing all this was only a first step in alleviating the problem. I had to spend several years watching myself repeat similar patterns, each time with a little less denial, and a little more awareness, self-forgiveness, and self-love.

The twelve-step programs are a brilliant and effective path to healing oneself. I believe that back in the 1930's when A.A. was created, it was truly channeled from a higher source. It continues to change and grow: In recent years, the work being done with A.C.A.'s (Adult Children of Alcoholics) is bringing to generations of people a new level of awareness.

We are all addicted to something, and these days there is at least one twelve-step program for everyone! Besides Alcoholics Anonymous, there is Al-Anon (for the spouses, families, or friends of an alcoholic or addict), Narcotics Anonymous, Cocaine Anonymous, Overeaters Anonymous, Co-Dependents Anonymous, Sex Addicts Anonymous, Workaholics Anonymous, and so on. A.A. and Al-Anon exist in almost every community in the country. (Look in the phone book if you want to contact them.) Meetings are free and your identity is kept confidential outside the meetings. My experience is that some meetings are better than others, but they all have an atmosphere of unconditional love and acceptance. The basic principles are there, and they work if you use them.

Personally, I am particularly fond of the first three steps and use them constantly in my life.

Here is my paraphrased interpretation:

1. I admit that I am powerless over this problem (or addiction, or situation). I've tried to solve it every way I know how and I can't seem to get anywhere. I feel stuck and helpless.

2. I recognize that there is a power in the universe that is greater than myself.

3. I turn this problem over to that Higher Power and ask for it to be resolved in the best possible way for my highest good and the highest good of all concerned.

I feel the twelve-step programs are a major spiritual path in the world today and will end up bringing more people to their own inner spiritual connection than any other source. In fact, I foresee a time when there will be meetings similar to twelve-step meetings in every neighborhood all over the world, and everyone will attend them. The atmosphere of honest sharing and true unconditional love will restore everyone to wholeness within themselves, and create a real sense of community with each other and with the world.

A.A. has remained pure because it has no leader. It seems to me that spiritual movements often become corrupted either by the ego personality of the leader, or by the ego personalities of the people who try to carry on after the original leader dies.

It seems fitting that the fundamental, grassroots enlightenment of the planet is coming through people who are willing to face their own deepest darkness. It is the way of Shiva—the tantric path. The journey into the light can only be made through the center of our darkness.

VOICE DIALOGUE

At one point, Tanha had described to me an interesting type of work her therapist was doing with her, and she gave me a booklet to read about the technique. The process was called Voice Dialogue, and it had been created by two therapists—Dr. Hal Stone and his wife, Dr. Sidra Winkelman. The minute I started reading about it, I felt the rush of excitement I only get when I know I'm in contact with something very important to me. It was the same feeling I had when I first went to Shirley's group.

Drs. Stone and Winkelman pointed out that we each have many different subpersonalities within us, and each subpersonality is a very real and distinct energy with its own function and its own needs, desires, and point of view. Frequently we are in conflict within ourselves because our different subpersonalities are in conflict with one another. Since we are usually more or less unconscious of this, we have no way of understanding or effectively resolving these inner conflicts. The result is that we have very little conscious choice about our behavior—we are simply at the mercy of whatever subpersonality happens to grab control at any given moment in order to take us in a certain direction.

Most of us have a certain group of subpersonalities that are in control of our lives most of the time. An opposite set of subpersonalities exists but is repressed and never finds much expression. Oftentimes, the repressed energies are struggling to come out, while the dominant selves are frantically trying to stay in control.

For example, a man who has led a very orderly, conservative life has dominant subpersonalities that are rational and responsible. He also has some repressed subpersonalities that would be freer, more spontaneous, and more emotional if they had the chance. Perhaps these come out occasionally, if he falls in love, or after he's had a few drinks, but usually his dominant selves will hasten to get everything back under control as quickly as possible.

Or let us imagine a woman who has been a wife and mother but begins to have yearnings to find a career. She may experience a painful conflict between her dominant subpersonality—the dutiful homemaker—and the newly emerging subpersonality, the career woman. The "homemaker" self may see the "career woman" as selfish and threatening to her family security, while the "career woman" may view the "homemaker" as old-fashioned and stuck. Neither one is right or wrong; both are important and necessary parts of the same person.

Voice Dialogue is a technique for identifying and getting to know our many subpersonalities. It gives us the opportunity to become fully conscious of all the different energies within us and eventually be able to have some choice about how we balance them. In Voice Dialogue work, a trained facilitator draws out and dialogues with the different subpersonalities, or "voices," of the client and helps the client establish a point of awareness from which he can objectively observe the various selves. It leads almost immediately to greater consciousness for the client, and an ability to start distinguishing one's own inner voices from one another. The work was derived in part from Jungian analysis, Gestalt therapy, Transactional Analysis, psychosynthesis, and other powerful therapies. In my opinion, Stone and Winkelman have taken some of the best parts of all these systems and combined and evolved them into a consciousness model that is the most clear, complete, and effective that I've ever discovered.

After first reading about Voice Dialogue, I became very ex-

cited because it clarified and brought together so many things I
was already discovering inside of myself. As I usually do when I
get excited about something, I immediately decided to find out
more about it. A friend who knew Hal and Sidra arranged for me
to meet them.

I loved them immediately and we have formed a deep friendship. Hal is a brilliant and innovative thinker, teacher, and therapist. Sidra is warm, wise, and extremely perceptive. Together
they have a lovely balance of male and female energies. One thing
that impressed me about them was their integration—they both
have a natural balance of their power and their humanity. They
have become wonderful friends and teachers to me and I'm very
grateful to have them in my life.

The more I learned about and used Voice Dialogue, the more
impressed I was with its effectiveness. It was amazing how the
process of really listening to the voices and allowing them to
express themselves fully immediately began to shift patterns that
I or someone I was working with had been stuck in for years.

One of the most important principles of Voice Dialogue work
is that the facilitator listens to each voice in an accepting, non-
judgmental way, no matter what the voice has to say. The facilitator functions somewhat like an objective interviewer, encouraging
the subpersonality to express its feelings and views fully and
freely. This encourages the client to begin to feel more accepting
of *all* of his or her selves, even those that may have been judged
"bad" or "wrong" in the past. It seems that the subpersonalities
primarily have a need to express themselves, to be heard and
understood.

In Voice Dialogue work, the facilitator does not try to change
or resolve anything for or with the client. He or she simply encourages all the selves of the client to express honestly and be
heard. The first step is for the client to become more fully aware
of all the different subpersonalities, some of which may be in
direct conflict with one another; he may have to live for a while
with the consciousness of his conflict and no immediate solution.

Resolution begins to happen naturally from awareness. As
the more dominant voices are allowed to express themselves fully,
they seem to relax a little and release some of their need for

control. This creates space for some of the disowned or less developed selves to begin to come forth and express themselves. This automatically begins to bring more balance and integration into the person's life.

Most importantly, as the client begins to hear his own subpersonalities expressed clearly and distinctly, he becomes aware of himself as an entity separate from all those voices. The facilitator helps him to develop what is called an "aware ego"—a part of himself that is not identified with any of the voices but can begin to have true conscious choice in responding to things in his life.

Hal uses this analogy: Before we develop awareness of the voices, it's as if our personality is a car, and the subpersonality that grabs control at any given moment drives the car wherever it chooses, while we remain locked in the trunk! After we become conscious of the process, our aware ego drives the car and makes a conscious choice to go in the direction a given subpersonality desires only if and when it is appropriate.

For example, when we are unaware, our rebellious child may grab the wheel of the car and start taking us down a self-destructive road with no conscious choice on our part. Once we have dialogued with the rebellious child, *and* the stern parent that it is rebelling against, and have developed some separation from both of them, our aware ego can make choices to do some of the things the rebellious child thinks are fun, but at appropriate moments, and without destroying our whole life!

Hal helped me understand the difference between consciousness and spirituality. Our spiritual nature is one aspect of ourself which we may either have disowned or developed. Consciousness is the awareness of all the aspects of ourselves. So you may be very spiritually developed, but if you are mostly identified with your spiritual self, you will probably be unconscious of many of the polarized energies within you, such as your instinctual and sexual self, your anger, or your very ordinary human self.

Many "new age" people are in this predicament; they have developed their spirituality but not their consciousness. A conscious person is one who is aware of and cultivates the development of all aspects of his or her nature.

Working with Hal and Sidra, I realized why I had found most

spiritual and psychological disciplines limiting: most of them encouraged the development of certain of our selves, but not all of them. That's why I'd had to go through so many different disciplines, as each one cultivated a different part of me. I was delighted to connect with Hal and Sidra's understanding, which embraces all the polarities, and integrates all the energies within us.

My experiences with Voice Dialogue confirmed the picture I had already developed of the relationship of soul and personality, and the crucial importance of the child self in the connection between the two. The spiritual essence comes into the human form and is born as a child. Since the child is extremely sensitive and vulnerable and the world is not a very safe or comfortable environment for it, the child immediately begins to develop defense and survival mechanisms—behaviors by which it can protect itself and get its needs met. These various mechanisms become the different selves, or subpersonalities, and together form the structure of the personality. Eventually the child, and the spiritual essence within it, usually become buried underneath the increasingly complex and rigid personality structure that's trying to protect it. It's a bit like protecting someone by putting them in a metal box and burying them a hundred feet underground. Effective protection, but extremely confining.

That is why it is so important to rediscover the inner child within each of us and allow it to express itself. As we discover the true feelings and needs of the child and begin to nurture and care for it consciously and effectively, we find that most of our old, rigid defense systems are no longer necessary, and we begin to relax and let go. The child comes alive and brings us emotional depth and authenticity, spontaneity, innocence, and joy. Through the child we reconnect with our soul, the essence of our being. Once again we are in contact with the universal spirit, the oneness of all life.

Hal and Sidra pointed out that we really have the energies of many different child selves within us. Not only do we have a child for every age that we've been, but each child has many different aspects. Here are some of them:

The *vulnerable child* is the emotional core of our being. It carries all our deepest feelings and is extremely sensitive, very loving, and easily hurt and frightened. It lives deep inside us and whether or not we are aware of it, it is constantly reacting to everything that is happening to us according to whether it feels safe and loved, or threatened, rejected, or abandoned. It needs a great deal of love, nurturing, and reassurance.

The *playful child* is the part of us that knows how to have fun. It just loves to play and laugh and have a good time and is always on the lookout for ways to do that. Some adults have managed to stay in touch with their playful child and they are the ones who know how to enjoy themselves (although if they are too identified with it, they may tend to be irresponsible).

The *magical child* is the part of us that is in touch with the unseen forces of the universe. It usually loves to be in nature, where it can relate to elves, fairies, and the spirits of plants and animals. Or it may like special implements and rituals, like magic wands, Tarot cards, crystals, etc.

The *creative child* loves to express itself freely and is not afraid to try new things. It loves to dance, sing, draw or paint, play drums or other musical instruments. It also loves to play games of imagination. In our culture the creative child often gets suppressed quite early by criticism from outside, and eventually by the inner critic.

The *wise child* is closely linked to the soul. It is the part of us that sees and knows the truth.

The challenge for all of us is to learn to consciously care for the needs of these inner children and protect them in the world. Then we can gradually let go of some of our old, unconscious patterns of defense. As the inner children flourish, they enable us to experience feeling and passion, intimacy, fun, magic, and our innate wisdom.

The cast of inner characters that most of us have developed as defense mechanisms to insure our survival in the world goes something like this:

The *protector-controller* is a conservative voice in us that tries to protect us by making sure we are following the proper rules and behaving in an appropriate way so as not to threaten our security.

The *pleaser* wants to make sure we always behave in a way that makes everyone like us, approve of us, and never be upset with us. It's an expert at psyching out what other people want and giving it to them.

The *perfectionist* has an ideal image of how we should look and act and wants us to live up to this ideal at all times. It's usually quite unaware that what it is asking for is often humanly impossible.

The *pusher* drives us to accomplish as much as we can. The pusher loves to make lists of tasks, and feels that the most important thing in life is getting it all done. Again, it's usually unaware that what it is asking for is impossible, and has no perspective on other things that may be important in a person's life, like intimacy or relaxation.

The *critic* keeps us constantly informed of what we are doing wrong, how we have fallen short, what mistakes we have made and are currently making or will probably make in the future, how terrible our appearance is, and generally how inadequate we really are. Many people's lives are unconsciously run by their critic (or a combination of perfectonist-pusher-critic). It is a great relief to begin to get some awareness and separation from your critic and realize that most of what the critic says is not necessarily true.

There are an infinite number of subpersonalities and everyone has their own variations. Here is a random sampling of some that may be developed in some people and relatively (or totally) disowned in others: the good mother, or father, the rebel, the hedonist, the rational self, the sexual self, the adventurer, the artist, the angry voice, the spiritual seeker, and so on.

Using the model of subpersonalities and Voice Dialogue work, Hal and Sidra do insightful and innovative work with relationships. One of their basic principles is that we are attracted to our opposite polarity—people who express the energies we have suppressed or disowned. Once we learn to recognize what disowned self the other person is mirroring to us, and use Voice Dialogue to get in touch with that part of ourselves, our relationship conflicts begin to shift and dissolve.

Their way of working with relationships is brilliant and helped me tremendously. Since I can't begin to explain their whole concept and way of working with people here, I highly recommend that you read their books, which are now published by New World Library: *Embracing Our Selves* (basic explanation of Voice Dialogue) and *Embracing Each Other* (Voice Dialogue as applied to relationships) by Hal Stone, Ph.D., and Sidra Winkelman, Ph.D.

Through Voice Dialogue I became aware that two of the primary selves I was identified with were my "mother" self and my "teacher-healer-therapist" self. My mother self's main function was to take care of other people around me. My teacher self was a kind of extended version of that, whose function was to try to care for, heal, and transform everyone in the world. The unconscious hidden motivation under all of it, of course, was to indirectly try to meet the needs of my own inner child. By loving and healing everyone else, hopefully they would all love me, and perhaps when they all grew up happy and healthy they'd finally be able to take care of me!

I saw how my unconscious identification with mother/teacher polarized other people into the child/student role. That was fine in an appropriate setting like a workshop, but frustrating when it happened with my friends, associates, and lovers! Not only was I stuck in this role with other people, there were other parts of my being that were not getting much chance to be expressed—my child, my adolescent, my "free spirit," my "ordinary girl," among others.

I learned that our primary identification doesn't change overnight; in fact it probably remains with us our whole lives. We tend to revert back to it for safety, especially in times of stress. But gradually we can become conscious enough to not be automatically stuck in it, and we can choose to allow other parts of us to express more.

I had been doing a lot of changing in the last couple of years and I had finally been allowing my vulnerable child to come out. The problem was that I still had very little aware ego present to make intelligent decisions about when to allow the child to come out and how to care for it. I had been bouncing back and forth between my mother self and my child self without much awareness. Through Voice Dialogue I began to develop an aware ego, and thus more consciousness of which subpersonalities were operating at any given moment.

Toward the end of the Creative Leadership Program, I asked Hal and Sidra to come and present a workshop to the group. The workshop was powerful and helped me realize what had been out of balance, not only in my life, but in the program. We had been so eager to explore the child that we had gone too far in that direction, without bringing in some balancing elements of adult rationality in order to protect the child in the world.

Through Hal and Sidra and Voice Dialogue, I began to find integration of all the things I had been exploring and discovering for many years, and of the many aspects of myself.

HEALING MY RELATIONSHIPS

The work I have done with Voice Dialogue has allowed me much more insight and perspective on my relationships. I can see how the men and women I am most attracted to mirror the parts of me I most need and want to get in touch with and express. I can also see how I get stuck whenever I unconsciously play out my old patterns, such as trying to meet the needs of my own child through taking care of others.

Through both the twelve-step work and the Voice Dialogue process, it has become obvious to me that changing our deepest patterns takes time and patience. Although I have many insights and breakthroughs day by day, and I can clearly see my own progress, it is taking me years to resolve and heal my core issues. Sometimes I have moments when I feel discouraged and wonder if I'll ever experience the fullness of freedom and love that I know is possible. Yet most of the time I feel excited, because I can see I am coming to know and love myself more and more, and that is being mirrored in all of my relationships.

Most of the difficulties in my relationships with friends have gradually worked themselves out with time and evolution. At one point Tanha and I got together to work through our issues. We used a structured communication process, something a friend had told us about which we modified to suit our needs. We used it off and on for several days, spending several hours at a time sitting and talking. It was a profound experience, and at the end of the process we both felt we understood each other on a much deeper level. We've used it since then when we need it, and I've used the same process with others. It is included in Part Four of this book.

My mother and I have continued to work through our difficulties. It became quite apparent that it wasn't working for us to try to deal with our issues within the context of the staff/family group—it just perpetuated the general co-dependent entanglement. We needed some objective facilitation, and so we began seeing a therapist, individually and together, whenever she was in the country. This helped considerably, and gradually our issues began to resolve themselves.

A major insight for me was that on a deep level, I had never really established a separate identity from my mother. Our bond was extremely strong. In my childhood of constant change, she had been my only consistent source of security, and since there was no one else in the family, we had been emotionally dependent on each other. Because her personality was so powerful, it was hard for me to find my own. Ironically, the values she had given me were so good that I never found reason to reject them and find my own, as most of my friends had done with their parents.

A big breakthrough for me was realizing it's really okay for my mom and me to disagree about some things. I don't have to agree with her point of view and I don't have to try to convince her that mine is right. We can both be right.

I had to work a great deal on my core co-dependency with my

mother—my unconscious tendency to take responsibility for her needs and feelings. I recognized that I responded to her habitually from guilt, which then led me to feel resentful. In fact I realized that I operated from a deep feeling of guilt in general. If anyone around me was in pain, a part of me automatically assumed it was my fault. That's one reason I was working so hard to heal everybody. Instead, I needed to learn to feel and respond to my own needs, to live life primarily for myself.

Once I realized this, I was better able to establish my own sense of myself and set my own boundaries with my mother and everyone else. As soon as I felt more secure in my identity and my right to live my life my own way, I was better able to love and accept my mother the way she is without trying to change her. In fact, I appreciate my mother for her love, her courage, and her commitment to her own process.

I have done a lot of inner healing work on my relationship with my father. I've allowed myself to experience all my feelings in relation to him—hurt, sadness, anger, and love. In recent times I've initiated some conversations with him about my childhood, in which we both have been able to express some of our feelings to each other. This has been very healing for me, and I think for him too.

Most important for me, I've been cultivating a relationship with an inner father—a strong, protective part of me that can watch out for my needs and make sure I use good judgment in taking care of myself. This feels very strengthening to me.

The healing I am doing within myself is being reflected in my relationships with men. I have spent time alone, getting to know and love myself deeply. Although I still have the same patterns and tendencies in relationships, I am more able to see what my real needs and desires are. Gradually I am learning to parent the child in me, to find out what she needs and wants and take responsibility for fulfilling those needs. Rather than unconsciously hoping and expecting that a lover will find out about my needs and fulfill them, I am learning to consciously ask for what I want, and find ways of providing it for myself if another person can't do it.

I realize that I have few living models for a truly good relationship between a man and a woman. In fact, I feel that human consciousness is making a leap into a whole new level of potential relationship and that what we have known in the past is far more limited than what will now be possible for us. I believe that we can have relationships that mirror and express all the love, depth, fun, passion, and ecstasy that is contained within our souls.

My inner guidance has given me a sense of what is possible for me and for all of us who are committed to this journey. I don't know how to get there—I can only ask the universe to teach me, moment by moment, step by step.

It is no accident that I was given the spiritual name Shakti. I am committed to a Tantric path—the journey which takes us through the deep, dark, unknown places in life, into the light of self-realization. In the Tantric tradition, Shiva and Shakti represent the male and female, seeking wholeness through their union. Relationship becomes the primary spiritual teaching, and I am a lifetime student of that teaching.

THE GARDEN ISLAND

Except for a brief change of planes on my way home from my trip around the world, I had not been in Hawaii since my trip to Japan when I was seventeen. So I was delighted when I was invited to do a workshop in Honolulu. My mother happened to be visiting a friend on the island of Kauai, so I flew over there to stay with her for a week before my workshop.

When I landed on Kauai I immediately felt like I was coming home, even though I'd never been there before. I was struck by the intense beauty of the place. It was so lush. It felt like the goddess energy, embodied in an island. As I swam in the turquoise sea and looked up at the green cliffs, I felt a combination of power and peacefulness. I felt myself being cleansed and healed by the frequent rain. When I left, I knew I'd be back again.

I went back to the islands several times in the next year, leading workshops and retreats on Oahu, Maui, and Hawaii, and taking some rare time for myself on Kauai. On one vacation to Kauai I found a beautiful big house available to rent for retreats. I decided to hold a three-week retreat there the following summer.

The Kauai retreat was a special experience. The setting was incredibly beautiful. The house was on a cliff overlooking a gorgeous, secluded beach. We did yoga early each morning, held our group activities, then in the afternoon went out and swam in the ocean, played on the beach, and explored the island. In the evenings we danced or sang or did creative artwork.

In group we worked with contacting and expressing the inner child. The setting was perfect for this: the island was beautiful and nourishing, and the house and the group felt very safe and cozy.

Something magical began to happen: it was as if all of our buried inner children felt safe to come out and play, and the entire group moved into a psychic space of innocence, openness, and wonder. Not only did the emotional closeness in the group deepen to a profound intimacy, but a lot of playful, creative energy emerged.

Since the house wasn't big enough for everyone to live in, many of the participants lodged nearby. A slumber-party atmosphere developed, and people spent the night with each other like kids. Most of the time a group of people spent the night together on the floor of the living room in the main house. Whatever sexual energy there was took on a very innocent and playful pre-adolescent flavor. No one was actually having sex—we were just having fun.

I was seeing the world with fresh new eyes—looking through the eyes of my inner child. Everything seemed especially bright and sparkly, and felt very real and alive. I knew this island was a magical place for me to connect with and express the essence of my being.

COMMUNING WITH THE ISLAND

The following summer I held another retreat on Kauai, but before that I spent a month on the island on my own personal retreat. It was a powerful time for me. I spent hours every day on a special secluded beach I had found there, the most beautiful and magical place I had ever been. When I was there I felt as if I had stepped back through time; in fact, I felt I was back at the *beginning* of time. I had the strange feeling that this was my place of origin. I noticed that the sand was the same color as my skin, and I had the image that I had actually arisen, or been created, from the sand on that beach.

Walking down the path to the beach, I always felt I was making the transition from my personality to my soul; I felt I was going into a deep meditation. On the beach, I felt in contact not only with my soul, but with a wonderfully primal part of myself. I felt completely aware of and in tune with my body, the way I imagined a beautiful animal would feel. Sometimes I felt like a nature goddess. And of course my magical child loved to come out and play there.

I love swimming in the ocean more than almost anything else (it's up there in the top three, along with making great love and dancing to fantastic music). The summer sea was warm and turquoise blue, and so salty I could easily float on my back and gaze up at the fluffy clouds drifting above. Sometimes dolphins would swim past me.

I found that as I swam, I began praying to the spirit of the island—to all the gods and goddesses there. I gave thanks for the opportunity to be in such a nurturing place, and asked for the island's blessing. I also asked to be shown if there was any way I could be of service here. In turn, I began to feel the island talking to me. Of course, I always have a strong skeptical voice that says, "What do you mean, the island was *talking* to you? You're just making that up!" Nevertheless, I have a strong and distinct experience sometimes of receiving information. As in this case, I oftentimes don't fully understand the information until later.

The communications from the island, which were rendered as much in feeling impressions as in words, went something like this:

> "I welcome you. I'm very glad you are here. In fact, I've called you here. I have much healing to give you. But I have also called you here because I need your help. I am fighting a great battle now. I have a strong fighting spirit that has never been conquered. But I need you and those you bring with you to align with me in consciousness. Through all of you I can bring my power into the human world."

These kinds of messages came to me often. The feeling which accompanied them was very strong, but I didn't fully understand what was meant. I sensed it might refer at least in part to the matter of development versus environmental protection that I knew was a major issue on the island. Kauai was being developed very rapidly, and there was fear it would soon succumb to the same kind of touristy overdevelopment that had happened on much of Oahu and Maui.

I wondered if I were meant to get politically involved and take an active part in this situation. Whenever I tuned in about this, I got the feeling there was nothing for me to *do* at the moment, just keep the lines of communication open and await further instructions.

A friend of mine who had lived on Kauai for a number of years mentioned that when King Kamehameha had conquered and united all the islands, he had never actually succeeded in conquering Kauai. The Kauaian warriors apparently had a particularly determined fighting spirit, as well as a natural fortress in the impenetrable cliffs of the Napali coast. That seemed to be an interesting corroboration of the messages I had received.

That summer (1987), those in new age circles were talking about the Harmonic Convergence—a two-day period in August that was said to be a particularly significant turning point in world consciousness. According to Jose Arguelles in his book, *The Mayan Factor*, this date had been predicted in the Mayan calendar for thousands of years.

I must confess that I have a very skeptical mind when it comes to most "new age" predictions and events. I do believe that we are in a new age, and I consider myself an integral part of the huge shift of consciousness that is taking place in the world. However, I find that many people involved in the new age movement have placed their spirit so far ahead of their form that they are very ungrounded. In Voice Dialogue terms, they have developed and identified with their spiritual and magical aspects, while repressing, or at least not developing equally, their human, physical, primal selves. They've tried to live in the light and leave the darkness behind instead of embracing both dark and light as the yin and yang of existence. They seem to me dangerously out of touch with physical reality.

I thought the Harmonic Convergence sounded like another airy-fairy spiritual good idea, and didn't pay much attention to it. However, as the time grew closer I had an interesting experience that seemed to be related to it. About two weeks before the predicted date, for about four days I felt that I was in an altered state of consciousness. During this time I channeled a lot of information and creative ideas relating to both my own personal life and purpose, and to the world at large.

I felt that not only the island but the Earth herself was communicating with me. She told me that this was indeed a major turning point in our relationship to her: We had reached the farthest extreme of our human journey into individuality and separation and were now turning back to move into integration and balance. She said it had been necessary to focus primarily on the development of male energy for a long time, and now the power of the feminine principle embodied in the Earth herself was reasserting itself in our consciousness. I got the image that Earth, our patient mother, was now shifting into a more demanding teacher. Most of the ideas expressed in Part One of this book came through at that time.

I'd already received the image that humanity, having left the innocence of the Garden of Eden in order to gain the wisdom of experience, would return to that garden to integrate the wisdom with innocence, the body with the spirit, and create a physical paradise on Earth. I had also received the name of my next book— *Return to the Garden*. And of course I had realized that Kauai was traditionally known as The Garden Isle. It occurred to me that I had been born in the Garden State, and was now returning to the Garden Island.

I felt that my own personal journey was tracing a clear and graphic microcosm of the macrocosmic journey of humanity. Early in my life I had separated from my spiritual essence, my child self, and my feminine side, in order to develop a strong male energy which allowed me to protect myself and accomplish my purpose in the world. That part of my journey was completed, and it was time for me to find integration with the parts I had buried. I had been drawn to the garden island to reconnect with my inner child, with my spiritual essence, my own feminine power, and with the spirit of the Earth. I knew that I was to make this my home, use the immense power here to heal my psychological wounds, and learn about and teach others how to live on the Earth.

FINDING HOME

In my gypsy existence, I had never owned a home. My mother had never bought a house, claiming it was too much of a hassle; she preferred to rent and have the landlord fix things that went wrong.

My accountant had been warning me for some time that I needed to buy a home unless I wanted to pay most of my income to the government. So I began looking for property on Kauai. I looked at a number of beautiful places and finally settled on what I thought was the right one. I didn't like certain things about it, but there were other features that persuaded me to go ahead with it. It had been on the market for quite a while, with no buyers. I made an offer, and began to think of the place as mine. At this point I was busy with the retreat, but in my spare time I fantasized about living on my new property and creating a retreat center there.

At the end of the retreat, however, I received word that another, better offer had come in on the house and it had been sold to another party! I was in a state of shock and disbelief. I had been so certain it was mine, and I was angry at the universe for misleading and cheating me!

I really didn't know what to do next, so I just put the whole thing on a back burner while I returned to the mainland to lead my workshops. The tentative plan was to move to Kauai in a year or so and spend about half my time there and half in California. My friends Tim and Ruby Star remained in Kauai to look for property for me.

I went back a couple of times in the next few months and

gradually it became very clear that the property I was meant to buy was the house that I had been renting for the retreats. Although it had been for sale, I had disregarded it because the house itself, while suitable for workshops, had a strange design. It was in a fabulous location, however, looking at one of the most beautiful views I had ever seen, with access to my favorite beach. Along with the house there were five acres of prime land. Tim Star, who was a building contractor, showed me how the house could be remodeled to be stunning. And it was being offered to me for an unbelievably low down-payment and great terms. Everything fell into place so perfectly and easily that I knew it was right. I regretted my earlier anger at the universe, since I could clearly see this was a far better choice than the original one I had made. In fact, I felt that I had been saved from making a big mistake.

Escrow closed in January of 1988 and I was the rather amazed owner of my first home—a beautiful property in paradise!

I still can't really relate to the idea of owning property. To me it seems an ironic joke that human beings can delude themselves into thinking they "own" a piece of the Earth. Hasn't it been here for millions of years already? If we don't destroy it, won't it be here for a few million more years at least? What a silly arrogant thought that we can possess and control it.

A few years ago a major hurricane hit Kauai and destroyed a lot of homes and property, but interestingly, no people. I delight in thinking that if Kauai gets too fed up with what human beings are doing to her, she can just call in another hurricane and destroy all our precious expensive buildings in a few seconds flat.

Rather than ownership, I instinctively relate to the idea of stewardship of land. It feels as if this land was given to me to care for. I believe that the spirit of the land itself is guiding me, and my job is to tune into its guidance through my own intuition, and follow its direction. So before I and my Kauai family build or plant anything there, we ask permission from the land and from the other beings that already live there. If we sense any resistance, we change our plans until the time feels right. This has led to some interesting and creative results.

Tim and Ruby Star worked out an arrangement to build their own little house on the property and become my caretakers. Dean came over to live in my house and handle the remodeling, and several other friends came to assist him. The plan was to expand the living room and add a whole second floor to the house. This was to be completed in about seven months—in time to hold our annual retreat there in August.

A year or so before, Dean and I had seen the movie *Witness*, a story about the Amish people in Pennsylvania. There is a beautiful scene where all the neighbors join together for a "barn-raising"; the men work together and complete the building in only a day, while the women cook a feast for them. I thought Dean was going to jump out of his seat with excitement. Afterwards he kept telling me this was his vision—a community of family and friends working together to build something beautiful. I felt the excitement of it too. Now we were enacting that vision! My house was going to be built for me by people who loved me and each other, and were committed to the vision of building a place of beauty, filled with the power of spirit.

The original idea was that this could be my home for about half the time—a place to do my writing, and a place to hold retreats. I had justified the financial outlay by the fact that I could make money by having retreats there. Technically the property was not zoned for retreats, but it had been rented for that purpose for years without posing a problem. There were no close neighbors who would be affected by it.

Shortly after I bought the place, the owner of the adjoining property began to build a home next door to me. I informed him of my plans to hold occasional retreats there, and since this was just his vacation home and he would occupy it only two or three months out of the year, I didn't foresee any objections. However, he became very upset and began protesting the idea of my holding retreats there at all.

One day I was feeling pretty discouraged about all this and I went down to the beach to meditate on what to do. I was thinking, "Oh my god, I've just bought an incredibly expensive house on which I am doing extensive expansion and remodeling and now I don't even know what I'm going to do with it!"

As I meditated, my guidance came to me very clearly and said, as if chiding me gently, "You're just upset because you think you have to *know* everything. The truth is, you have no idea what you are going to be doing with this space. But that's okay because *I* know and I will let you know at the appropriate time. It's all going to be very new, a new phase of your life. That's why you can't see it yet. So follow your creative impulses and trust what falls into place easily, and what is blocked. You are doing exactly the right thing; go ahead and build your big, beautiful house. You are building your new structure, one that's large enough to express your spirit. Build your dream house, to house your dreams."

I was much reassured by this. I realized how much I needed to have my own personal retreat away from the world. My habit had always been to invite as many other people as wanted to come into my space, and help them heal themselves! Now I began to wonder how much I really wanted a lot of other people in my space. I realized I needed my own home.

MANUELA

While my Hawaii home was being remodeled, I went back to California to supervise the Shakti Center and do my usual workshop tours. I was still living in the same apartment in Marin County where I had been for several years. I was tired of living alone, and something occurred that turned out to be one of the most fortuitous things in my life.

Many years before, I got to know a woman named Manuela who went to some of the same workshops and groups I attended. I had always liked her, and every now and then we bumped into each other. Manuela was about my age; she was born in Italy, had married an American writer, Joel, and had lived in this country for twenty years. I knew that Manuela was a multi-talented person, and that in recent years she had worked as a secretary/housekeeper/assistant to a well-known filmmaker and his wife. I had always kept in the back of my mind the idea that she might someday work for me in that capacity.

I heard through the grapevine that she was no longer working for the filmmaker. I was feeling totally overworked, as usual, and knew I needed more help and support, so I called Manuela and asked her to come to work for me.

As it turned out, Manuela and Joel were just going through a separation, and she needed a job and a place to live. So she moved in with me and became my personal secretary, housekeeper, advisor, close friend, and overall "left-hand woman" (Kathy Altman still being my "right-hand woman").

Manuela's presence in my life turned out to be exactly what I needed. Not only did she help me enormously with every practical aspect of my life, she became a wonderful friend. We were both going through a painful time in our relationships and were able to give each other an enormous amount of emotional support.

Manuela is a beautiful woman, with all the characteristic Italian intensity and passion for life. She speaks with a charming accent and so much expression and animation that I love listening to her talk about anything; even a mundane topic becomes excitingly alive when Manuela is discussing it. She's intuitive, artistic, capable, and one of the most conscious beings I've ever met. I can ask her advice about anything, ranging from how to decorate my apartment, to what kind of process to do in a workshop, to what to do about my boyfriend, and she almost always comes up with the right answer.

Manuela expresses the archetype of the gypsy wise woman, and I've discovered that it's great to have one around the house! She has been my close companion for the last two years, and I foresee a long creative future together. She is a blessing in my life for which I literally give thanks every day.

BURNOUT

In spite of Manuela's considerable help and support, I grew more and more exhausted. I had been working so hard for so long, putting out so much energy to so many people without knowing how to replenish myself, that I was finally beginning to run on empty. The pain of my relationships had completely drained me emotionally; I began to understand how co-dependency, like alcoholism, can literally kill you. I fell into a pattern where I woke up very early every morning and could not go back to sleep, so I was getting only a few hours sleep each night. I was too busy to get regular exercise, and for the first time in my life I put on extra weight.

I was thirty-nine years old, facing my fortieth birthday on September 30th. I have always been healthy and vital, with a slender, youthful body. The prospect of aging had never been a reality to me at all. I literally assumed it would never happen to me, and I think this is a natural assumption of youth. In my case, it was reinforced by my metaphysical belief that it is possible to transcend what we have come to know as the aging process to a large extent by living in harmony with the life force rather than in opposition to it. I always figured that by the time I got around to aging, I would be so enlightened it would no longer be an issue!

Imagine my surprise to suddenly confront the fact that I was about to turn forty. I simply couldn't believe it. Inside I felt like I was still about seventeen. To make matters worse, my body was definitely changing. The quality of my skin was different. I had put on ten or fifteen extra pounds and was feeling flabby.

I remember that my mother, who had been thin all of her early life, had started gaining weight when she turned forty. I realized I had always had an underlying fear that this would happen to me as well. I could feel that my body was following that unconscious conditioning and starting to act it out.

I felt strangely helpless to do anything about this. It was as if my body was living out its deep programming, both personal and societal, and I had to go through it. I couldn't stop it, change it, or short-circuit the process. At the same time, I sensed that some of the anxiety around this issue would clear up, but I really didn't know how or when.

I knew I needed a break, so I especially looked forward to going to Kauai for the summer. I would have a month or so to relax before our summer retreat.

I arrived on Kauai determined to spend the summer resting

and healing myself, and being as good to myself as I could be. I wanted to swim in the ocean, sunbathe, get my body in shape, help with the completion of my house-remodeling, and celebrate my new home on the island.

KAI MANA

The scene at my house was totally chaotic. Dean, Tim, Ruby, and the rest of the crew had all been living in the house while remodeling it for the past six months. During much of that time, various parts of the roof had been torn off. When I arrived, the entire front wall of the living room was gone. Cats, birds, chickens, and flies roamed freely through the house. Tools and paint cans were strewn everywhere. Since the carpet was going to be replaced anyway, nobody bothered to clean anything up off the floor.

Because I am usually compulsively neat and organized, I would have expected to be miserable with all this disorder. Surprisingly, I loved it. It was like a child's fantasy house, where you could make as much of a mess as you wanted and not have to bother to clean it up! I claimed a bedroom and managed to keep that a relatively orderly refuge, but I enjoyed surrendering to the utter confusion that reigned everywhere else.

Dean was in his element—the knight building a beautiful castle for his queen. Tim Star had created a wonderful design, and Dean carried it out with superb craftsmanship, with the assistance of the entire family. I was grateful for the special feeling of having my home created with so much care by people who loved me.

By mid-August it was completed, and it was truly magnificent—simple and spacious, with lovely views in every direction. My bedroom is the most beautiful room in the world, as far as I'm concerned. Light, airy, and peaceful, it looks out over the beach and the ocean.

We held a celebration in which many of my friends came over from the mainland to stay for a week. We performed a ritual asking for a blessing from the island and from the spirit of the land itself. We decided to name my new home "Kai Mana." Loosely translated, it means "ocean of power." We asked that Kai Mana always be a place of healing and transformation.

It felt like our tribe was gathering in its new (or ancient) home. I had an image that we were like knights of the round table, who were being called together to perform a special mission, to manifest our visions into physical reality.

TRISTAN

As a child I had always dreamed of having an Arabian horse; since I had room for a horse on my property, I decided that one good thing I would do for myself was buy the horse I had always wanted! I thought having a relationship with a horse might temporarily replace some of my need for a relationship with a man. I found an Arabian horse ranch on the island, and bought a beautiful dark bay (chocolate brown, actually), pure Arabian gelding named Tristan. Since Tristan was the name of a knight in a very romantic story—Tristan and Isolde—it seemed appropriate. He was only three years old, intelligent and spirited, and absolutely gorgeous!

Fortunately, the owner of the ranch and the trainer, Sarah, were very helpful. I had only a small amount of experience with horses and had no idea how much there was to learn. As it turned out, Tristan was quite a handful for me. Sarah gave me lessons while she continued to train him. It was challenging, but I loved it. There was something that felt very familiar and natural about relating to horses—like a past-life memory. When I brushed Tristan's mane, I always felt like a Native American warrior with my pony.

Ironically, my relationship with Tristan turned out to very similar to my relationships with men! In certain ways he was like the men I was attracted to—young, smart, gorgeous, inexperienced, a bit wild, and hard to handle. He has demanded a great deal of time and energy, and I've had to face a lot of my fear in relationship to him. And I've learned many of the same lessons with him as in any other relationship: how to set clear boundaries, communicate my needs directly and clearly, and keep my own power instead of giving my power to him. It's been challenging and fascinating, and I guess it just proves that you can't avoid your process no matter what you do.

One day I was out riding Tristan. I had grown very confident with him, and was riding alone on a remote trail. Tristan was galloping along pretty fast, when something startled him and he shied violently. The next thing I knew I was on the ground. When I sat up, I was covered with blood that seemed to be dripping from my face. No bones seemed to be broken, so I got up, caught Tristan, and rode him back to the ranch where I kept him for training. Nobody was around, so I put him away, got in my car, and drove home. I was in shock, though I didn't know it. When I walked into the house everyone gasped; I looked in the mirror and saw that my entire face and chest were caked with blood.

Dean drove me to the hospital where I had six stitches taken in a deep gash on my face (the only stitches I've ever had). It has healed well, but I now have a prominent and visible scar on the right cheekbone.

The interesting thing is when I first hit the ground I remember having the feeling that I was undergoing some type of warrior's ritual. It was as if some part of me knew I had to go through with it, and was proud of and almost exhilarated by it. I think of my scar as a battle scar and I really rather like it.

A few months later, Tristan caught his leg in a barbed wire fence and cut the entire leg open down to the bone. It took several months and a lot of care, but he has now healed beautifully. He, too, apparently went through an initiation and carries his battle scar.

FORTIETH BIRTHDAY

It became increasingly clear to me that I needed to change my entire way of life. I needed less work and responsibility, and more healing, nurturing, and fun for myself. I felt I had spent years giving to the world, and now I just wanted to give to myself.

I decided to take a break from leading workshops after my birthday. I wanted to spend several months on Kauai relaxing and writing my new book.

As my birthday approached, I kept getting a strong feeling that I had made some kind of agreement before I was born that I would spend the first forty years of my life focusing on making my contribution to the world, and after that I would be free to live my life for myself. I have no idea whom I made this agreement with, or even if this is true, but I knew I was reaching a major turning point in my life. I felt as if I was walking through a door into freedom.

On my birthday I spent most of the day on the beach, walking and meditating. I asked myself what I wanted from the next year, and I received the simple and powerful answer, "To love and be loved. I just want to love and be loved."

I knew that this next year would be a time of letting go of much of the external complexity of my life and coming more into the simplicity of my heart.

TRANSFORMATION

The six months I've spent living on the island while writing this book have been wonderfully healing for me. For the first time in many years I have not led any workshops or dealt with the public at all. I have rested, relaxed, and gotten plenty of sleep. I've found peace and quiet and stillness. Most of my attention has gone into myself rather than anyone else. And I have been nurtured by the incredible beauty of nature around me.

I've spent time alone , surrendering to my feeling of loneliness and emptiness and moving into it rather than running away from it. While this is initially scary and difficult, each time I do it I find that the emptiness inside is filled by the power of my own soul, which feels incredibly rich and full.

In surrendering to the feeling of emptiness, I am allowing myself to discover the power of the feminine aspect of my being. In emptiness there is openness, a receptivity which has the power to attract whatever it needs and desires. I am attracting more and more love into my life, from many sources.

I've had a relationship that's been good for me, with a beautiful and dynamic young man—a talented rock 'n roll guitarist. This relationship has been an important part of my healing. While it has some of the same characteristics as my previous relationships, it has some important differences too. We've each been so committed to our own process that we've been able to move quickly through the patterns in which I've previously gotten stuck. As a result I've been able to receive the transformational gifts of the mirroring process.

I understand now why I've been constantly attracted to younger men in recent times. I instinctively felt that I needed a vital young male energy to replenish and renew the life force I had drained by giving out so much and taking care of so many. I knew on some level that a virile young man could transform me from the mother I had become into the young goddess I felt like on the inside. In tantric exchange, I would give my wisdom and power.

This older woman/younger man exchange is a very natural and powerful relationship. It seems especially appropriate at this time, when the power of the goddess is coming forth. However, it is a tricky process, especially since society's current standards do not favor this model. If the woman is not careful, she can remain in the mother role and the transformation does not take place.

In this relationship, I have received an energy I needed. His physical, passionate vitality has renewed my connection with my own. He has mirrored a number of previously disowned energies, which now I'm in touch with.

Being with him has taught me how to express more of the primal, physical energy that goes after what I want. It's the opposite of taking care of other people. There is also a warrior energy that isn't afraid to get angry if I feel I'm being treated unfairly. There is a rebel aspect to it, too, which helps me cut through my tendency to please other people and allows me to do what I feel, regardless of what others may think. And my fun-loving adolescent and playful child are starting to come through, too.

I have a strong soul connection with this man, but our relationship at this time has reached completion of its initial form. I don't know exactly how it will manifest in the future. I find this openness suits me perfectly right now. Rather than trying to control things, I'm learning daily to surrender my life to the guidance of my higher power and trust the unfolding process of my journey.

I feel a deeper, stronger connection to my own essence, and that is being reflected in my relationship with my body. My energy has been replenished and renewed, and I feel healthy and fit again. The energy I've released in my relationship is bringing a new strength and vitality into my being. I feel young and very alive.

I've always been sensitive to my body's food needs and eaten very consciously. I don't follow any rules, but just eat whatever I really want and try to stay aware of what feels healthy and nurturing to me. I've noticed in these last few months that my needs are changing and, for the most part, I'm eating a simpler and healthier diet than ever before, especially when I'm on the island. I love to walk and swim, and try to do so every day. (Then again, some days I just need to loaf.)

One day recently I had an interesting experience. It was a gorgeous sunny day and as I was walking along the beach, I saw a friend of mine doing yoga. She is a lovely woman—tall and slender with long, dark hair, and quite accomplished at yoga. As she moved into various postures there on the beach, she looked so stunningly beautiful that I literally had to stop and catch my breath.

As I watched her, I felt myself move into an altered state of consciousness. I saw a radiant energy emanating from her and suddenly I experienced a new level of aliveness that I'm beginning to move into. I realized there's nothing I have to try to do about it, just follow my experience which will continue to lead me in that direction. I did feel a strong desire to do more yoga, which I have acted upon. Yoga was the first step I consciously took on my spiritual path in this lifetime, and it is still a powerful one for me.

I have a strong desire to dance again as well. I've done it sporadically over the years, but now I would like to focus on it more directly. My body and spirit need and want to dance.

NEW DIRECTIONS

I will probably do only occasional workshops in the future. I feel my form of expression is shifting. I would like to move into creating transformational theater experiences, incorporating music, dance, drama, and comedy, with the whole audience participating. For several years now I've had the feeling that through theater we could accomplish the same types of powerful changes in our lives that we do in workshops and it would be even more fun!

I have continued to tune into the spirit of Kai Mana and to ask it to direct me toward its purpose. I realize Kai Mana is meant to be primarily my personal house—a retreat for me, my spiritual family, and invited guests. Strange as it must seem to many of you, it is a big step for me to recognize my need for a private home and put it ahead of my desire to provide a place of healing for others. It is strongly symbolic of the fact that I am finally setting personal boundaries and taking care of myself first.

I have also received guidance to create a larger retreat center somewhere else on the island. I would like this to be a beautiful healing place where people can spend a few weeks or months, and go through a complete transformational process—physical, emotional, mental, and spiritual. I believe this is meant to be a place where people can learn to live in a new way, in tune with their own spirit and with the spirit of the earth. I envision that people will come here to heal and learn, then take their experience back home with them in order to teach others and help them heal.

Rather unexpectedly, I have begun to get involved in the politics of the island. Until very recently the island was controlled by an extremely pro-development government, and commercial development is threatening to quickly demolish much of the natural beauty of the island. Recently a new mayor was elected, a lovely and powerful young woman who is dedicated to good planning and finding an appropriate balance between necessary growth and preservation of the beauty of the environment.

She and others who are concerned about finding that balance have a tough fight on their hands. The developers are strong and determined and have nearly limitless funds. And there are many ingrained patterns in the government and the community that are difficult to change. But more and more people are beginning to realize that the integrity of the island is being seriously threatened, and they are starting to fight back.

Since learning more about the situation, I understand more clearly the messages I have received from the island. I believe Earth herself is calling out to those of us who can hear her, asking us to protect and defend her in every way we can.

One thing that seems clear is that we can't be effective in protecting the environment and transforming humanity's attitude toward the earth by coming from the victim position and blaming those who currently wield most of the power. We must empower ourselves and find effective ways to challenge them. It has become apparent to me that in the political world, money has a great deal of power. So, for the first time in my life I am becoming interested in making and/or attracting money. I want to use it to help accomplish the kinds of changes I believe need to be made in this world.

This island is my primary power place at this time. I think it has a certain destiny as an environment where great transformation can take place, and will be a model for the rest of the world. I believe there are many such powerful locations on the earth today. Some are quite remote, while others are in the middle of cities.

I urge those of you who are moved by what I've shared here to attune yourself to the earth wherever you are, and find out what she has to say to you. Then ask your intuition to guide you step by step on your personal journey into the new and conscious world we are creating here on Earth. Together, let us return to the Garden.

THREE

OUR JOURNEY

A FABLE

In the beginning there was only Woman, radiantly beautiful, existing in a state of serene bliss. One day Woman became aware that she desired a mate, so that she could experience the giving and receiving of love as well as the contentment she felt within herself. Since she was one with the creative principle, her thought and her desire immediately brought into creation a male child that was born from her. Since he was young and new, she nurtured and cared for him.

He grew to be a strong and handsome young man. Woman adored him and he adored her. But he was not yet powerful enough to be her mate. He needed to experience life.

So one day he kissed her goodbye, and vowing to return soon, he set out to seek wisdom and power in the world.

He encountered many obstacles and dangers. Often he was frightened and uncertain of what to do. But he would think of Woman, and his love for her would inspire him to meet every challenge.

He traveled far and wide, through many lands. He encountered and conquered many fearsome creatures. He gained confidence in himself. His body grew strong and powerful. He developed a reputation far and wide, and all the other creatures respected and feared him.

As he ventured farther and farther from his original home and became preoccupied with his adventures, the memory of Woman began to fade. Eventually, he forgot her completely, swept up in the thrill of his own power, which he found to be greater than that of any other creature on earth.

He looked only for his next challenge, his next conquest. He killed many creatures and claimed their territory for his own. He was relentless in his quest, pushing ever onward.

One day he was chasing a creature who had eluded him and he came to the edge of a cliff. His momentum was so great that he almost fell over the edge, but managed to stop himself just in time. He realized with a shock that he had reached the end of the earth. For the first time in a long time he felt lost and frightened. He couldn't go any farther and had no idea what else to do.

Night was falling, so he lay down to sleep by the edge of the earth. That night he dreamed of Woman. He saw her beautiful face and form, and felt her loving presence. He awoke with a start, yearning for her. He realized he had forgotten the very meaning and purpose of his life, and in so doing had lost his way and almost destroyed himself. He knew he had fulfilled his quest, and it was time to return home and find his mate.

As he made his way back in the direction from which he'd come, he found that the way was hard and long. No longer driven by his relentless quest for power, he had to face his own limitations. He was humbled, and in his humility he found wisdom. As he made his way more slowly, he was able to observe and understand many things about himself and about life.

He discovered that many of the creatures he had heedlessly slain had become demons who now blocked his way and threatened him fiercely. He found that if he ran from one, it pursued him relentlessly. If he killed it, it multiplied into a thousand who continued to pursue him. The only way to deal with the demons was to stop and befriend them, to discover the teachings they had for him, and to include them in his entourage. Once they were accepted and included, they used their power to help him on his journey homeward, which then became that much quicker and easier.

Finally one day he arrived home. He was tall and strong, with a face weathered and softened by experience and wisdom. He was surrounded by all the beasts and demons he had tamed and befriended, who were now his advisors.

Woman had been waiting and yearning for him for eons of time. She had known of all his adventures and sensed that he had forgotten her. She had feared he would never return. She had come to know pain, sadness, loneliness, fear, and anger, and had delved deep within herself to find trust and faith. Her experiences had strengthened her, yet deepened and softened her as well. Her beauty was so great that when he saw her, his heart stopped for a moment in his chest.

He knelt in front of her and promised to love and protect her and be with her always. She knelt facing him and promised in turn to always love and nurture and be with him.

Then they both rose and embraced.

Slowly they began to dance. . . .

FOUR

YOUR JOURNEY
Meditations and Practices

CONNECTING WITH YOUR INNER GUIDANCE

Find a comfortable position for meditation, either lying down on your back, or sitting with your spine straight and well supported. Close your eyes, take a deep breath and as you exhale, relax your body deeply. Take another deep breath and as you exhale, relax your mind and let your thoughts float away. Continue to breathe deeply and slowly, relaxing your body and mind.

Now take another deep breath and as you exhale, imagine moving your awareness into a very deep place inside of you. With each breath, keep going deeper and deeper. Come to rest in a quiet place in the core of your being. Take a few moments just to *be* in this peaceful place inside.

Imagine that in this deep place within you, you can connect with the wisest part of yourself. This is the part of you that knows everything you will ever need to know and can guide you step by step along your path in life. All you need to do is ask for it and this inner wisdom will begin to come to you.

Ask right now what your inner guidance wants to say to you or remind you of. Ask that it be something simple, something you can easily receive. Then relax and be receptive to whatever thought, feeling, or image that comes to you and feels right.

If nothing comes, you are probably blocking the process by

trying too hard. Don't make a big deal of it. You might even feel
as if you are making things up at first. If so, go ahead and make
it up! It still comes from inside of you. Some people find it helpful
to imagine they are talking to a very wise man or woman who is
giving them the guidance they need.

The more you practice asking for your inner guidance and
trusting what comes to you, the easier and more reliable the
process becomes. You can ask specific questions or ask for help
with specific problems. If you don't get an immediate answer
from within, you will find that it will come to you later in some
form—a thought or feeling, a dream, a book, a remark someone
makes to you that triggers a feeling of inner knowledge.

AWAKENING YOUR BODY

When you wake up each morning, lie in bed for a few minutes
and tune into how your body is feeling and how you feel emotionally. Tell yourself that you love and appreciate yourself as you are,
and that you accept all your feelings and emotions as a natural
part of life. Tell your body that you appreciate it for being there
for you.

Slowly get up, and get a large glass of fresh water and drink
it slowly, thinking of how the water is cleansing and replenishing
your body. Don't drink or eat anything else for a few more minutes.

Put on some music that suits your mood. Slowly and gently
begin to move and stretch your body. Ask your body how it wants
to move and let it show you what feels good. Think of moving
different parts of your body like your head, shoulders, arms and
hands, hips, legs and feet, so they all get a chance to "wake up."
Then move your whole body freely to the music in whatever way
feels good to you. When you're ready to stop, lie down and relax.
Feel the life energy pulsating through every cell of your body.

EXPLORING MALE AND FEMALE ENERGIES

Find a quiet place, either indoors or outdoors, where there is enough space to move around and where no one will disturb you.

Stand in a comfortable position with your knees slightly bent. Breathe slowly and deeply. Imagine the nurturing, female energy of the earth coming up through the soles of your feet and filling your whole body. Begin walking or moving around, feeling the female energy in your body. Allow yourself to feel open, sensuous, receptive, intuitive, powerful. Sense your connection with everything around you. If you are a woman, imagine that you are a goddess. If you are a man, imagine that you have a goddess within you. Move your body with the energy of that goddess.

When you feel complete with this, come to a standing position again. Slowly release the female energy from your body, back into the earth. Then imagine that you are taking in male energy through every pore of your body. Let yourself be filled with this male energy. Begin walking or moving around with this energy. Allow yourself to feel strong, clear, focused, powerful. Sense your individuality, your distinctiveness from everything around you. If you are a man, imagine that you are a god. If you are a woman, imagine that you have a god within you. Move your body with the energy of that god.

Notice the difference in how your body feels with the female energy and the male energy. Be aware of how differently you relate to your environment from each perspective. Each is important, each is powerful. Play with these different energies in your life, calling them in when you need them. Experiment with bringing both of them in at the same time to see if you can experience a balance of the two.

DISCOVERING YOUR INNER CHILD

Find a place to meditate that feels very quiet, safe, and comfortable, where you know you will not be interrupted. Sit or lie down, arranging blankets and pillows around you so that you feel especially cozy and comfy. If you are preoccupied or tense, play some soft, light, peaceful music and breathe slowly and gently for a little while to allow yourself to relax. Then begin the meditation.

Close your eyes and begin to imagine that you are in a beautiful place somewhere out in nature. You are walking along a path, seeing, feeling, or sensing the peacefulness and beauty of nature all around you. You come to a particularly lovely, magical spot and you begin to explore it.

You become aware that a little way off is the figure of a small child. You start to move toward the child, and as you do you become aware of whether it is a boy or girl, about how old it is, how it is dressed, and what it is doing. As you move closer still, you can sense how the child is feeling—if it is sad, contented, afraid, angry, excited, curious, pensive, or whatever. Being careful not to startle the child, begin to approach and make some contact with it. How you do this will depend on the mood and activity of the child. Trust your intuitive feeling about the best way to get to know this child. You may want to talk to it, touch or hold it, join in the game or activity the child is engaged in, explore together, or just sit quietly. Let the child indicate to you what it wants and what is appropriate.

At some point, ask the child either in words or telepathically if it has something it wants to tell you, or some message it wants to give you. Be receptive to hearing or receiving its answer. Ask the child what it wants or needs from you, right now or in your life in general. Receive the response, whether it's in words or some other way.

The child has a gift for you—something it wants to give you. Let yourself now receive this gift. Whatever it is, it's symbolic of what the child's message is to you right now.

When you feel it's time to leave, let the child know that it can either come with you, or remain here in the safety and seclusion of this beautiful place. If it chooses to stay, let the child know that you care for it, and that you will come back to visit as often as you can. If it wants to come with you, take it by the hand or pick it up in your arms, and begin to go back up the path.

Once again become aware of your body and of the room you

are in. Very slowly and gradually open your eyes. Feel the energy and presence of the child, inside you or with you.

You have made contact with some aspect of your inner child. If you found it difficult to do, it may be because your inner child is not yet ready to emerge. Try the meditation again every now and then, and when you are ready it will happen. You may feel like you are just making something up. That's fine, because it's some aspect of your inner child that's making it up! The child you meet may be playful, magical, or hurt, frightened, or angry. Trust whatever comes as being the part you need to be in touch with right now. If you do this meditation often, and continue to work with the child, you may find that things change.

Some people initially meet a sad or upset child who has never had its needs met. As you begin to love and reparent that child consciously, the child may become happier and more playful. Others meet a playful child to begin with, and perhaps later when it's safer, a more vulnerable child may reveal itself.

Meeting your inner child is the beginning of creating a loving, responsible relationship with that part of yourself. Do the meditation often, and establish a regular connection with your child. Find out what the child needs and wants, and begin to give it as much as you can, both in meditation and in your life.

Treat your inner child like you would a real child that you loved and cared for. Go into a toy store and let your child choose a stuffed animal and/or a toy it *really* likes. You may feel foolish, but you can always pretend you are buying it for some other child! Make a habit of including some activities in your life that your inner child really enjoys, like swinging on swings, riding a bicycle, playing with trains or trucks or dolls, going to children's movies, the circus, an amusement park, or the beach.

Find out what feels nurturing to your child, and include more of this in your life. Most children need lots of loving contact with people they feel care about them. Often they need touch and affection. In these busy times, many inner children need more peace and quiet and rest. Children usually like animals and are nurtured by contact with them. You may realize that your dog or cat or goldfish is your inner child's best friend! And most children love to be out in nature.

Remember books that were special to you as a child, and reread them. Read yourself bedtime stories. If you have a willing partner, take turns reading each other bedtime stories and tucking each other in bed!

As you give your inner child the love and fun it needs on a regular basis, you will feel a great deal of healing take place inside of you. Life will gradually become richer and more enjoyable.

EXPERIENCING THE FOUR ELEMENTS

Find a comfortable place, outdoors if possible, but indoors is fine, too. Lie down on your back on the ground or on the floor. Make sure you have a rug, towel, or cloth underneath you and a small pillow or rolled towel under your knees, if necessary, to make you comfortable. Breathe slowly and deeply and allow your body and mind to relax completely.

Feel (or imagine) the earth underneath you, supporting your body. Let yourself receive this support, and feel your body relaxing more and more as you trust the earth. Imagine your body becoming earth—strong, steady, and serene.

Now imagine that it begins to rain. Feel the moisture on your earth body. Imagine that the rain washes the earth into a river. Feel yourself dissolving into water—flowing and swirling, loose and free.

Imagine yourself splashed up and evaporating into the air. Now you are floating lightly and freely as a soft breeze, almost without form.

Feel the hot golden rays of the sun shining through you. Let yourself merge with that heat and become that bright fire.

Now that you have experienced each of the elements—earth, water, air, and fire—come back and simply feel your body, relaxed on the ground or floor. Think about how your body and all of creation are made up of combinations of these four elements.

CONNECTING WITH A SPECIAL PLACE

Find a natural place on Earth that you love. (If you are not in touch with loving any place, find a place you like.) It could be your back yard or the park across town or your grandfather's farm. It could be a beach or forest somewhere, or a resort where you vacation. Find a place that's accessible to you now, and go and spend some time there.

Spend time tuning into the place. Do whatever you want, but let it be something that allows you to feel, see, and be aware of the place itself rather than distracting you from it. You might walk around and just look at everything you find there, or lie down on the ground and feel the earth underneath you. Imagine you are very young, and explore the place the way an innocent child would.

Find an appealing place to relax and meditate. Get in a comfortable position. Take a few deep breaths and relax your body and your mind. Imagine that you are tuning into the spirit of this place. (You may feel as if you are making the whole thing up and that's fine—go ahead and make it up.)

Ask the spirit of the place if it has anything it would like to communicate to you. The communication could come to you in words or some other way—through images or feelings. Ask if it needs or wants anything from you, or if it's having any problems it would like you to know about. If so, is there anything you can do to help?

Also, ask the place for anything you would like to receive from it, such as serenity, nurturing, healing, power, or whatever it is. Allow yourself to imagine receiving exactly what you want from being there.

Continue to cultivate your relationship with this place on a regular basis, in whatever way feels best to you. If you become aware that it is having difficulties, see if there is anything you can do on a practical level to help. You will find yourself well-rewarded by your relationship with your special spot on Earth.

FINDING A POWER OBJECT

Go out in a beautiful natural setting and find a comfortable place to sit for a short meditation. Breathe deeply, relax your body and mind, and let your awareness drop into a deep, quiet place inside of you. Ask your inner intuitive self to guide you to an appropriate power object.

Then get up and take a leisurely walk, looking around you and observing everything you see on the ground and in your surroundings. Pick things up and look at them if you feel drawn to them. At some point you will find an object that feels meaningful or powerful to you. It could be a rock, leaf, feather, seashell, pinecone, or anything else.

Sit down and meditate again, holding your power object. Ask it what meaning or significance it has for you. Trust whatever comes into your mind after you ask this question. Let yourself receive the message or feeling from your object.

Take it home and put it in a special place in your house. Take a moment to acknowledge it in some way each day.

DISCOVERING YOUR POWER ANIMAL

Get in a comfortable position for meditation. Breathe slowly and relax deeply. Let your awareness move into a deep, quiet place inside of you, and imagine that you are connecting with your inner guidance. Ask to discover your power animal.

Now imagine that you are walking through a forest or jungle. You see and/or feel the presence of many animals all around you. At some point you encounter an animal who has particular significance for you. Ask it what its message is to you and be open to receiving it. This animal may talk to you in words, or telepathically, or it may indicate what it wants to say to you through its actions. Trust whatever intuitive feelings come to you, and relate to the animal accordingly. You may feel you are making the whole thing up, and that's fine, too. Just continue to do so.

This animal represents a certain kind of power or wisdom. Let yourself receive its special gift to you. Know that this animal is now your special friend or ally. Call on it whenever you need its energy.

TREE MEDITATION

Find a special tree. Sit under it, or climb up and sit in it, or stand close to it and put your arms around it, finding whatever way feels right to relate to it physically.

Close your eyes and relax into a meditative state of mind. Imagine that this tree is either a mother, father, brother, or sister to you. Talk to it in your mind and tell it how you feel about it. Then let your mind be quiet, and let yourself receive the energy from this tree. You may find it to be nurturing, or strong, or wise, or perhaps humorous. Trust whatever relationship you feel with this tree.

If you live nearby, come to see your tree often. You may find it to be a very comforting and loving friend.

ROCK MEDITATION

Find a big rock that's smooth enough to sit on, lie on, or lean against. Relax deeply, and feel your body against the rock. Feel how strong and firm the rock is. Notice how cool or warm it is. Think about how ancient it is and how long it has been sitting in this one spot. Pretend that you are the rock and try to imagine what it would be like to sit so calmly and still for hundreds, thousands, or perhaps millions of years. Let yourself absorb the serene, powerful energy of this rock.

ASKING FOR A BLESSING

Whenever you do anything in nature or related to the earth, take a moment to ask for a blessing from the earth and from the plant, animal, and other nature spirits in that place.

If you are building a home or any other structure, or planting a garden, first create a little ritual. Let part of the ritual be a request for a blessing from the place itself, and cooperation from all the beings that already live there—the plants, insects, animals, and so on.

Ask to be guided in the correct and highest development and use of the property. Then trust your intuitive feelings about how to proceed. If you encounter obstacles, let it go for the moment and ask for further guidance. Then keep following your ideas and impulses. The plans that are not right will get seriously blocked; the right ones will usually happen easily.

Remember that we can never truly "own" a part of the earth. We are the caretakers, and the place itself will let us know what it needs and wants.

TELLING YOUR STORY

At some point in our lives, we need to tell our story. This is a powerful process which can bring awareness, integration, and completion to certain phases of our lives.

Try to write the story of your life. This could be as simple and brief or as long and detailed as you want. If you are not inclined toward writing or typing, tell your story into a tape recorder. Or do it in the form of drawings or paintings, or dance it. Another alternative is to simply tell it to a friend, a group, or a therapist (one you feel comfortable with, and who has the time, interest, and patience to follow through with this).

In telling your story, don't worry about dates and specifics—focus on important events and feelings. Remember that you are doing this *only* for yourself, for your own satisfaction and self-knowledge. You are not trying to impress or please anyone else, or do anything according to any rules or standards. Do it in a way that feels right to you.

By keeping a journal or another type of record of your experiences, telling your story can become an ongoing process.

WRITING WITH YOUR OTHER HAND

Writing with your nondominant hand (your left hand if you are right-handed, your right hand if you are left-handed) is a powerful way to gain access to the deeper or more disowned aspects of your being. You can ask this hand to represent your soul or essence, your inner child, or your creative being. Then ask that part of you what it has to say to you and let your nondominant hand write it.

For example, ask your inner child to write you a letter telling you what he or she wants to tell you or needs from you. Then write the letter with your nondominant hand and sign it with the name you were called as a child.

Or you can write questions from your personality with your dominant hand, and write answers from your soul or your higher self with your other hand.

For more information on this technique, read *The Power of Your Other Hand* by Lucia Capacchione.

COMMUNICATION PROCESS

This is one of the best processes I've ever found for resolving difficulties in communication and relationships. This can be done with just the two people involved, but at first it may be best to have a facilitator present as well, especially if the problem is serious or long-standing and there are a lot of emotions involved. Once you have learned to do it successfully with a facilitator, you can easily learn to do it without one.

If you have a facilitator, it should be someone who can remain objective and impartial, and who both participants trust. The facilitator makes sure that the participants follow the rules of the process and stay within the structure, and does not offer any comment or attempt to help the participants solve the problem.

The only other requirements for the process are:

1. Both participants need to be *willing* to work things out and desirous of resolving their problems.

2. A pleasant and comfortable physical space in which to do the process where there will be no interruptions.

3. At least one-and-a-half to two hours. Less time may be required but it's important to allow for more in case it's needed, and especially if it is a serious conflict. Also, it is important to set another time in the near future to continue the process if time runs out before you feel resolved. People often grow to enjoy this process so much that they choose to continue it on a regular basis.

A fundamental human need is knowing that someone we love understands how we feel. Frequently in conflicts both people are desperately trying to be heard and understood, while neither one hears or understands the other. The communication process, if done correctly, almost ensures that both people will end up feeling that they've been listened to and understood by each other. This dissolves most of the emotional charge, and allows other aspects of the conflict to be resolved much more easily.

To begin, find comfortable sitting positions and face each other. You should each have a notebook and pen handy. (In the section that follows I'm writing it as a man and woman in conflict, but of course it can be any two people.)

Each person starts by making a brief statement of their goal or desire for this session. For example: "My goal is to feel you understand my side of this" or "I want us to resolve all this hurt and anger so we can feel loving toward each other again."

Once these goals have been stated, you begin the main part of the process as follows:

One person takes his (or her) turn first. He simply talks about the problem, stating his feelings and his point of view about it as clearly as possible. It's best to concentrate on talking about the main issues and the feelings involved rather than focusing too much on the details of what happened, who said what, etc., unless that feels important. He should talk for about five to ten minutes.

Meanwhile the second person listens carefully to everything being said and tries to understand and remember the main points of what is said. Most people find it helps to take notes, although some find it too difficult or distracting. The important thing is that the second person listens to the first one carefully enough so that she can repeat back to him the essence of what has been said.

When the first person finishes his initial statement, the second person repeats her understanding of what has been said (she need not get the details, only the main points about how he sees and feels about things). She is not agreeing with him, but simply letting him know she has listened to and heard his point of view. If she has misunderstood what he said or has forgotten anything important, he can then explain the corrections, which she also repeats until he feels satisfied that she has heard him accurately.

Then she takes a turn and spends five to ten minutes stating *her* perspective on the problem and how she feels about it. He listens carefully, taking notes if he finds that helpful. When she comes to a good stopping point, he repeats back to her the essence of what she has said. She then has an opportunity to clarify or correct his statement until she feels he has accurately reflected her point of view.

Then he takes a turn again, taking another few minutes to discuss the issue, while she listens and then repeats what she's heard. Then it's her turn again.

Continue taking turns until both people feel they have had a chance to say everything they need to say, and feel that the other person has heard them and repeated accurately the main essence of what has been said.

At first, you may experience great difficulty in doing this. It is very hard to sit quietly and listen to another person's perspective when you have a lot of upset feelings about what they are saying. There is a very strong temptation to jump in and correct, contradict, or argue with them, because you just *know* what they are saying is wrong, inaccurate, unfair, etc. (That's why the facilitator may need to be there.) If you can exercise the patience and discipline to follow the process, you will find it gets easier after a while, because you *do* get a chance to express your feelings and have the other person listen to your side of it.

Remember that in listening and repeating what's said, you are not in any way agreeing with what another has said. You are simply letting the other person know that you hear what he or she is saying. It may help to imagine that you are an objective reporter, interviewing someone and taking notes on what they say.

When you are the one talking about your side of things, try to bring out the deeper underlying feelings as much as possible, instead of focusing on superficial details. Once our deeper feelings are expressed and heard, we usually begin to feel some resolution of the problem.

Here is a brief, simplified example of one round of the process:

First person: I was really angry that you came home so late last night and didn't even call me. Sometimes I feel like you are *so* inconsiderate. Especially after I *told* you I was going to make a special dinner. And then when you came in you hardly even talked to me. I just can't stand being treated this way.

Second person (repeating essence): So you were very upset that I came home late and ruined the special dinner you fixed. You think I'm terribly inconsiderate for not calling.

First person (correcting): The worst part was that you didn't communicate with me when you came in.

Second person (repeating correction): The hardest thing for you was that I didn't talk to you much when I came home.

First person: Yes.

Second person (taking his turn): This is just another example of what I'm always having to deal with. I have a really tough day at the office, I'm completely overwhelmed with problems and demands, I don't have a minute to get my thoughts straight, and then I come home and have to deal with your anger. It sure would be nice to walk in and get some affection for a change. Sometimes I don't even *want* to come home because I don't know what I'll have to face.

First person (repeating): You're saying that you had a really terrible day at work and then you felt like you came home to another problem. It seems to you like this happens a lot. You wish I would be warmer to you when you come home.

Second person: Yes, I guess that's about right.
And so on.

This process can have a very powerful effect in resolving the hurt feelings that are underneath most of our conflicts. Of course, it is not a magical solution to serious relationship difficulties. If you find that you can't follow the format, or that it doesn't help you much, I strongly recommend seeking professional counseling. I think most of us need help with our relationships at certain times, and there is no substitute for a good therapist or facilitator.

For those of you who do find it helpful, you may discover that doing a short form of this process regularly keeps major problems from escalating.

THANKING THE EARTH

Each day when you first get up, take a moment to look out your window or walk out into your yard and observe the beauty of nature as it is that day. If you live in a city apartment with no yard or trees, you can do this with your house plants, or lean out a window and look at the sky.

Say thank you to the earth mother and to all the elements. Give thanks for another day of life. It is a precious gift.

ENVISIONING THE GARDEN

Get in a comfortable position for meditation. Close your eyes, take a few deep breaths, and relax your body and mind.

Pretend you can project yourself a number of years into the future. Imagine that you have done a great deal of inner healing and self-transformation. You have come to love and express all aspects of yourself in a balanced, integrated way. As a result, you are wise, powerful, loving, and radiantly alive. The male and female energies within you are developed and balanced, and your inner child is expressed fully and freely. You are in tune with and guided by your own soul.

You have intimate, honest, exciting relationships with others who mirror your wholeness. You are expressing yourself creatively, doing work that you love. Imagine as many details as you wish about your living situation and your personal life. Let it be your highest vision for yourself.

There has been a great transformation of consciousness in the entire world. The human race is now living in harmony with itself, with the other species, and with our planet. Many of the institutions and structures that were no longer in tune with the needs of the planet have been dismantled or transformed. Governments now run effectively for the highest good of everyone. People live daily lives that are filled with the natural richness and passion of earthly existence, fully attuned to their connection with their spiritual source. Fill in your own creative ideas and details about all of this.

Imagine the Earth restoring herself to her natural balance. More beautiful, varied, abundant, and magical than ever, she is truly a wondrous place to live. Humankind has developed wisdom and consciousness and has thereby returned to the Garden.

SUGGESTED READING

Embracing Our Selves by Hal Stone, Ph.D., & Sidra Winkelman, Ph.D., New World Library.
An introduction to Voice Dialogue.

Embracing Each Other by Hal Stone, Ph.D., & Sidra Winkelman, Ph.D., New World Library.
Using the principles of Voice Dialogue to understand and heal our relationships.

Maps to Ecstasy—Teachings of an Urban Shaman by Gabrielle Roth. New World Library.
A guide to your primal, healing self by an extraordinary teacher.

Getting the Love You Want—A Guide for Couples by Harville Hendrix. Henry Holt & Co.
An excellent book on relationships. Read it even if you aren't part of a "couple."

Healing the Shame That Binds You by John Bradshaw. Health Communications, Inc.
A powerful book on recognizing and healing the pain from childhood.

A Primer on Adult Children of Alcoholics by Timmen L. Cermak, M.D., Health Communications, Inc.
One of the clearest and best on the subject.

Co-dependent No More and *Beyond Co-dependency* by Melody Beattie. Harper & Row.
Two good examples of the many current books available on co-dependency.

Focusing by Eugene Gendlin. Bantam Books.
Describes a simple and powerful technique for getting and staying in touch with yourself.

If You Want to Write by Brenda Ueland. Graywolf Press.
Should be read by everyone who wants to live a more creative, fun life—delightful!

The Power of Your Other Hand by Lucia Capacchione. Newcastle Publications.

Speaking of Siva—Translated by A.K. Ramanujan. Penguin Classics.
Poems to Shiva written by twelfth-century Indian saints. A personal favorite of mine.

The Tarot Handbook—Practical Application of Ancient Visual Symbols by Angeles Arrien. Arcus Publishing Co.

Diet for a New America by John Robbins. Stillpoint Press.

The Power of Myth by Joseph Campbell. Doubleday.

The Universe is a Green Dragon by Brian Swimme. Bear & Co., Inc.

The Presence of the Past by Rupert Sheldrake. Times Books.

Kinship With All Life by J. Allen Boone. Harper and Row.

Behaving as if the God in All Life Mattered by Michaelle Wright. Perelandra, Ltd.

Nature: The Other Earthlings by James Shreeve. MacMillan.

A Sand County Almanac by Aldo Leopold. Ballantine Books.

Restoring the Earth by John J. Berger. Doubleday.

Talking With Nature by Michael J. Roades. H.J. Kramer, Inc.

On Nature—Edited by Daniel Halprin. North Point Press.

Life in the Balance: Companion to the Audubon Television Series by David R. Wallace. Harcourt Brace Jovanovich, Inc.

The Immense Journey by Loren Eiseley. Random House.

The Unexpected Universe by Loren Eiseley. Harcourt Brace Jovanovich, Inc.

For more information about ways to help restore and clean up the environment, please write:

NEW WORLD LIBRARY
P.O. Box 13257
Northgate Station
San Rafael, CA 94913

Also By Shakti Gawain

Books

Creative Visualization
Creative Visualization Workbook
Living in the Light
(with Laurel King)
Reflections in the Light—*Daily Thoughts and Affirmations*

Cassettes

Creative Visualization
Living in the Light
Developing Intuition
Meditations with Shakti Gawain
—*a series of four audio cassettes:* Contacting Your Inner Guide,
The Male and Female Within, Discovering Your Inner Child,
Expressing Your Creative Being.

Video

Creative Visualization Workshop Video